Options Trading Crash Co

The Ultimate Guide to Generate a Passive Income from The Financial Market. All You Need to Know to Make Money Online Using Proven Strategies

Table of Contents

Introduction

Options are contracts that grant the owner the right to purchase or sell a sum of underlying assets at a predetermined price but not the duty to do so, at or before the expiry of the contract. Options can be bought with investment brokerage accounts like most other asset groups.

Options are powerful because they can expand the portfolio of an investor. This is done by adding revenue, security, and even leverage. Depending on the case, an optional scenario is usually suited to the target of an investor. A common example would be to use options as an efficient safeguard against a falling stock market in order to reduce downside losses. There may also be options for generating recurring profits. They are also often used for speculative purposes, such as wagering on stock courses.

No free lunch is provided with inventories and bonds. There are no different options. Options trading entails such risks which must be understood by the investor before trading. This is why you normally see a disclaimer similar to the following while trading with a broker:

Derivatives options

Options belong to the broader category of so-called derivatives securities. The price of a derivative depends on or comes from the price of something else. Options are financial equity instruments — their value is dependent on the price of some other assets. Calls, posts, future assets, forward assets, swaps, and mortgage-backed securities are examples of derivatives.

Call and Put Options

Options are a form of safety derivative. An option is a derivative since its price is intrinsic to something else's price. If you are buying an option contract, you are given the right to purchase or sell a basic asset at a fixed price, but not before a certain date.

A call option allows the holder to purchase a stock and a put option allows the holder to sell a stock. Consider a call option to pay for a potential order.

Call Option Example

A future homeowner is witnessing a new trend. This person may want a right in the future to buy a house but will want to exercise it only after certain projects are developed around the city.

The future house buyer will profit or not from the purchase option. Imagine that the developer will purchase a call option for $400,000 at any time in the next three years. Ok, they should, you know that as a deposit which cannot be reimbursed. Of course, the developer will not grant such an option free of charge. The prospective purchaser must make a down payment to secure this right.

This cost is known as the premium for an option. It is the price of the contract for the option. In our home example, a deposit of $20,000 could be paid by the buyer to the developer. Let us claim that two years have passed, and projects have now been constructed and zoning approved. The buyer practices the option and buys the house for $400,000 as it is the bought deal.

This house may have doubled its market value to $800,000. But as the down payment is locked at a predefined price, the purchaser pays $400,000. Now the zoning approval does not come through until year four in an alternative case. This is one year after this option expires. Now that the contract has expired, the home buyer must pay the market price. In this case, the developer retains the initial $20,000.

Put Option Example

Now consider an option as an insurance policy. If you own your house, you probably know how to buy home insurance. A homeowner buys a policy to protect his home against loss. For a while, let's say a year, you pay a sum called the premium. The policy has a face value that provides cover to the insurance holder in the event of harm to the house.

What if your asset was an investment stock or index instead of a home? Likewise, if an investor needs protection on the S&P 500 index portfolio, they can buy options. An investor will fear that a bear market is close and may not lose more than 10% of its long position on the S&P 500 index. If the S&P 500 trading at $2,500, for example, they will buy an option to sell the index at $2,250, at any time in the next two years.

When the market crashes by 20% (500 points on the index) in six months' time, it sells the index to $2250 for a combined loss of just 10%, which amounts to 250 points. In reality, even if the market drops to nil, the loss is only 10% if this placement option is maintained. Again, buying the option carries a cost (the premium), and if during this time the demand is not reduced, the maximum loss on the option is just the premium.

What is financial trading?

Financial trading is no different from any other method of trading, namely the purchase and sale of assets in order to make a profit. Here we talk about the main principles, participants, and financial trading markets.

The purchase and sale of financial assets is financial trading. It is done in two ways: through an exchange or through the counter OTC (Over The Counter). An exchange is a highly organized market where a particular form of the tool may be traded. You may, for example, trade US shares on the New York Bourse (NYSE). When you exchange through the counter, you trade between two parties directly. For instance, purchasing a CFD contract from a trading agent such as IG.

What is traded in financial trading?

Financial tools, like shares, forex, or bonds, or derivatives like CFDs, futures, or options can be exchanged. The desired result, regardless of the instrument being traded, is always the same: to make a profit. If you buy and sell an instrument at a lower price, you make a profit. You would lose if you sell an instrument for less than you purchased it.

Who trades?

Millions of businesses, people, organizations, and even governments are trading at the same time on financial markets. But what is a trader? What is a trader? A trader is described as a person who purchases and sells financial instruments in order to make a profit.
Some traders adhere to a specific instrument or asset class, while others have different portfolios. Some do a lot of research before putting a company, while others read charts and look at patterns. However, both companies have one thing in common – they all take risks. Risk is a core concept for all financial trading types. No matter which tool is traded, who trades, or where the trade takes place, balancing potential benefit against risk is crucial for an effective trading strategy.

Which markets are tradable?

Thousands of financial markets, including bonds, indices, cryptocurrencies, and forex, are to be exchanged. IG offers over 16,000 trading markets, with over 12,000 securities, 90 currency pairs, and 30 indices.

Trading Vs investment: what's the difference?

The distinction between trade and investment is whether you are making a profit and owning the asset. Traders try to benefit by buying low, selling high (long), or selling high (short), typically over the short or medium term. Investors will also seek to benefit from low-priced, but long-term, purchases of shares. They can also seek revenue in the form of a dividend.

CFD trading is a common trading tool, although investors can trade ETFs (Exchange Traded Funds). When you sell products, you do not own the actual asset, but you own it when you trade in shares.

Rules and Customs

You have to be sure that you know the trading rules after you chose your broker. While margin standards are imposed by federal law, trade settlement regulations, and restrictions on movement openly, brokerage companies often have much tougher rules for their customers. You must check with your broker for more rules imposed by your selected company.

The rules on stock trading come under the competence of the Federal Reserve, which in Regulation T lays down its stock trade regulations. The rules set out in Regulation T shall include margin accounts, broker-trader accounts, stock sales, expanded securities credit, and other securities market-related factors.

Margin Requirements

Regulation T of the Federal Reserve shows how much you can borrow from a marginal account in order to buy new shares on the margin. This initial condition allows you to borrow up to 50% of the cost of the new shares.

If the stock price rises, the balance of equities increases. If the inventory price falls, the equity balance falls. Your margin balance stays the same, $10,000 in each case. The only way to reduce the margin balance remaining is by depositing additional cash into your account or selling stock shares.

When your share price increases, your balance of equity increases and you can use increased equity as leverage to borrow extra capital to purchase additional stock shares. You will buy up the value of the increased balance of equity, which increases the margin balance.

However, NASD rules govern the minimum equity position allowed on your account if your equity balance falls. The minimum current value of all marginalized securities is 25 percent if one is a pattern day trader. Some brokers might need more.

For a trend day trader, if the stock's total value falls below 13,332, then your original $10,000 portfolio's equity balance is less than 25 percent of the remaining total value. Mathematics is simple: 25 percent of 13,332 dollars is 3,333 dollars. Your cash balance remains at $0 and still remains at $10,000. To calculate your equity balance of $3,332 subtract $10,000 from $13,332.

You can never meet a margin call as a trader. You should instead close the offending location (s). An extraordinary event can cause the stock value to fall below the amount owed by your outstanding margin loan. Your broker will close your positions if this takes place, but you still have to repay the debt.

Not all inventories can be purchased at a margin and not all inventories can be used as collateral. Make sure you understand your broker's margin criteria.

Settle Trades

If you make an order to purchase a stock, the transaction must be settled in three business days. This period of settlement is called T+3. The brokerage company shall be paid for all securities you purchase no later than three days after the execution of the trade. Many brokers today need cash before placing the company unless you have a margin account. If you sell a stock, it is likely to be kept on your brokerage account, and on the day of settlement it is taken out of the account. The trading options and government securities on a T+1 settlement cycle mean that these transactions settle on the next trading day.

Free Riding

Free riding means that you have to pay for the stock before the stock is available and since it takes three days to settle a stock transaction, you can in principle potentially buy a stock and then place an order for the stock to be sold before it actually settles. In reality, you can buy and sell a stock without cash for the late payment period.

This is a challenge with the cash account. Although many swing and day traders turn stock buying and selling fast, they usually trade on a margin account and avoid the issue. However, day traders and swing merchants must have sufficient cash or purchasing power in their accounts to cover all inventory transactions.

You have enough money in your account.

The company respects your commitment in good faith to make full cash payments for the security before you sell it.

If you ever buy and market security before the payment period (T+3) is complete and without enough cash in your account, a brokerage company may make an intraday loan extension but exposes the company to an increased risk. Most brokers need active traders to purchase and then sell securities to carry out these activities on a marginal account during the settlement period.

You may freeze your account for 90 days if you have not entered into any kind of credit agreement with your broker.

Trader's Mindset

Being a trader does not only mean better tactics and more thorough analyzes, but also a winning mentality. What distinguishes a winning trader from a loss, according to several studies by traders:

- Winning traders do NOT devise stronger trading strategies

- Winning traders are NOT wise

- NOT winning traders do better study of the market

What distinguishes a winning merchant from a losing merchant is his psychological thinking.

Most traders falsely assume that all they need to do when they start trading is to find a great trade strategy. After that, all they have to do is come every day to the trading market, plug in their great trading plan, and the market will start pouring money into its account at once.

Unfortunately, it's not that convenient, as all of us who have ever traded have discovered. There are many traders that use clever, well-designed trading strategies and systems that are still losing money daily, rather than making money.

The only traders that consistently win the trading game are those who have established the psychological mentality that makes them consistent winners. The world of trade needs certain values, behaviors, and psychological characteristics.

Attitude towards the markets and yourself

Business perceptions and opinions include stuff like the assumption that the market is dishonest against you. Such negative – and wrong – views can have a major effect on your trading ability. If you look at the competition as being there to get you, then you don't really look at it and can't expect to critically analyze market opportunities. The market is totally indifferent – whether you make money or lose money doesn't matter. Our confidence in ourselves is critical to the psychology of trade. One personal attribute of almost all winning traders is self-confidence. Winning traders have a powerful, fundamental conviction that they can become winning traders – a confidence that is not shaken seriously by a few, and some, losing trades.

Many losing traders, by comparison, have extreme, squabbling doubts. Sadly, if you regard yourself as a loser merchant, slandered by poor luck or something, the conviction appears to be self-fulfillment. Traders who doubt their ability frequently hesitate to press the button and start trading and often lack strong trading possibilities. They still want to cut profit short, too afraid that the demand will always turn against them.

Winning traders value the fact that even their best market forecast often does not fit potential price shifts. Nevertheless, they have general confidence in their capacity as traders – a trust that makes it easy to start trade whenever there is a real opportunity.

A winning trader's main characteristics
The best traders share the same psychological attributes, including:

They all take chances comfortably. People with very low-risk tolerance, who cannot tolerate losing trade, do not win because losing trade is actually part of the trade game. Winning traders should embrace the confusion inherent in trading emotionally. Trading is not like investing your money in a guaranteed return savings account.
They are able to adapt rapidly to changing market conditions. They don't fall in love with their business research and "marry." If price action shows that they can adjust their views on likely future price movements, they do so without hesitation.
They are disciplined and can look critically at the market regardless of the impact of current market actions on their balance of accounts.
They are not too happy about winning trades or too desperate about losing trade. Winning traders monitor their emotions instead of being controlled by their emotions. They make the necessary efforts and take the necessary measures to be independent traders who operate with strict rules on money and risk management. Winning traders are not ruthless players. Before joining any exchange, they carefully measure potential danger against potential rewards.
One of the psychological characteristics of winning traders is their willingness to embrace (1) risk and (2) your mistake more frequently than you do in initiating business. Winning traders recognize that management of exchange really is more important than the study of the market. What decides the gains and losses also are not so much about how or when you enter a business, but much more about the way you run a business when you are in it.

Understanding how the Trading works

Winning traders are familiar with the difference between 'bad trade' and trade that loses money. This is a crucial point to recognize. Just because you lose money in a trade does not mean that it's a horrible trade – it just means that it's a trade that's losing. What makes a trade a good trade is not whether it is won or lost –commerce is good, as long as it provides greater potential benefit than risk, and whatever the odds or chances of success is in your favor. If you take a trade for good reasons and handle the trade well while you are there, then it is a good trade, even if you end up losing. (In contrast, even though a trade makes money, if it has not been initiated for good reasons and has the favorable risk/reward ratio, it is evil, even though it might have turned out profitable.)

Winning traders work on the assumption that they would be profitable overall if they continue to make "successful businesses" as described above. Losing traders wrongly classify any trade that loses money as a "bad business" and any trade that makes money as a "good business" regardless of whether a fair basis exists for doing business – which leads to bad and long-term loss of trade. The evaluation of trades purely on the basis of whether they win or lose just makes a random reward like the play on a slot machine.

The Winning trader's upside-down attitude

One reason loss is so common among traders is that many behaviors and values that serve us well in life do not work well in the trade profession. Many traders are ignorant of this fact and lack a clear understanding of the trade.
We are taught to avoid dangerous circumstances in our ordinary everyday lives. However, trading means taking risks.

Trading is a risk-filled undertaking necessarily.
Winning traders who truly embrace the risk of trading have the opportunity to join without hesitation and close a trade just as quickly when it doesn't work. They are not burdened by the emotional pain which causes them to lose focus or trust because of a trade that does not work.
Traders who have not mastered this approach to trading are motivated by emotional responses to win or lose trade and have not really recognized that trading is a business that carries risks. They do not take the best trading decisions, because they are not in accordance with reality.
Trading – and performance – places a huge demand on us, namely the demand that we retain trust in the face of continuing trading volatility on the markets.
In the trade profession, one of the main elements of success is the reality of what we are engaged in.

Winning habits of a trader

Winning traders monitor and assess their trading success periodically. You recognize that trade is a skill that can only be learned over time by diligent practice.
Traders winning are versatile. You are not ego-invested in your company. They will still critically view the market and quickly throw aside business ideas that don't work.
When winning traders see a real opportunity to benefit based on market analysis and trading strategy, they do not hesitate to risk capital. They don't gamble money ruthlessly, however. Still mindful of the probability of wrongness, they are strictly managing their risks by limiting their losses.

Understanding that the market cannot be predicted

Winning traders are aware of and agree that there is no reliable market analysis technology or strategy, which can unfailingly forecast price fluctuations, in the end, is unpredictable. Since they are well aware of this, they are vigilant to look for evidence that their analysis is wrong, and they will easily change their trading stance if they see such signals.

By comparison, once traders have entered into a trade, they tend to look only for market action which confirms their right and minimizes or rationalizes all market measures that appear to be inconsistent with their study. They also end up wasting too much time and in unnecessarily high losses.

Trader's Freedom and Discipline

Trading is essential without borders, the market is totally open. You can purchase or sell, join or leave at any time. Basically, there are no laws that force you to open or close a trade at a certain price or time. Despite the fact that one of trading's main attractions is full liberty to take our own decisions – to essentially do whenever we want – the only way we can always succeed in doing business is by imposing a series of rules to regulate our trade and by enforcing those rules in strict discipline.

What is the problem? What's the problem? The problem is that unconsciously, we all love the right to do what we want and hate that we have laws and constraints, including those of our own making.

Self-discipline is essential if a trade is to be won. Sadly, self-discipline is generally the most difficult discipline. Most of us do well to obey the rules put on us from outside us, such as, for example, a sign for "No Parking," than to respect the rules we make for ourselves. We seem to be one more attitude: "Well, I have taken over the law, so I am free to violate it." This is theoretically valid, but it is not an attitude that will serve you well in your trade.

The solution is yourself

Losing traders erroneously conclude that controlling the market itself is the secret to winning. They don't face the fact that the market cannot be regulated. The market can't be regulated.

You should regulate yourself and what you do with regard to the activities of the market. Winning traders know this and make more efforts to master themselves and their business activities than to master market analysis. It is not helpful to analyze the industry. The quantity of available knowledge and the amount of different technological or fundamental indicators is almost infinite. Moreover, at some point in time what is important may be totally meaningless at another point in time.

All too many details can be sorted out and inevitably not be handled perfectly. A trader spends more time mastering himself and his business skills.

The Importance of Trading Psychology

For successful trading on the financial markets, several skills are needed. They have the opportunity to analyze the basic values of a business and evaluate the course of a stock pattern. However, none of these techniques is as critical as the trader's thinking. Emotion, fast thinking, and discipline are all components of what we might call trade psychology.

Two key emotions need to be known and controlled: fear and greed.

Snap decisions

Traders also have to think quickly and take swift decisions, with short notice stocks in and out. They need a certain presence of mind to achieve this. They will need the ability to adhere to their own business plans and know when to make gains and losses. Emotions can't just get in the way.

Understanding Fear

When traders receive bad news about a certain stock or the economy in general, they are naturally afraid. They can overreact and feel obligated to liquidate their holdings and stick to the cash without taking any more risks. If they do, they can prevent some defeats, but they can also lose some gains.

Traders must consider fear: a natural response to a perceived danger. It is a challenge to their profit potential in this situation.

It may be helpful to quantify terror. Traders should only understand what they fear and why they fear it. But the thought should take place before the bad news, not in the center. By thinking about it in advance, traders would know how they automatically interpret and respond to events and can overcome the emotional response. This is of course not simple, but it is important not to mention the investor for the health of the investor portfolio.

Overcome Greed

On Wall Street, there's an ancient saying that "pigs get slaughtered." This relates to the habit of greedy investors being too long a winner to bring the last price up. Tendency reverses sooner or later and the selfish get trapped.

Greed is not easy to conquer. It also depends on the instinct to do better, to get a little bit better. A trader should be able to understand this impulse and create a trading strategy, not whims or intuition, based on practical thought.

Setting Rules

When the psychological crunch arrives, a trader has to build rules and obey them. Set criteria for joining and exiting a company based on your risk-reward tolerance. Set a benefit aim and avoid the loss to get emotions out of the equation.

You may also determine which particular events should cause the decision to buy or sell a stock, for example, the release of a positive or negative income.

The overall sum that you are prepared to win or lose in a day should be set wisely. Take the money and run if you reach the profit mark. If your losses reach a default, roll your tent up and go home.

Anyway, you'll live to trade another day.

Conduct research and evaluation

Traders must be specialists in inventories and markets that concern them. Keep up with the press, learn and, if possible, participate in trading workshops and conferences. Ensure the analysis process takes as much time as possible. This includes learning diagrams, talking to management, reading business journals, and carrying out other background work, like macroeconomic analysis or market analysis.

Knowledge may also contribute to overcoming fear.

Keep versatile

It is critical that traders remain versatile and consider experimenting occasionally. For instance, you can consider using risk mitigation options. One of the easiest ways to learn is to experiment (within reason). The experience can also lead to reducing the emotional impact.

Finally, traders should review their own success regularly. Besides examining their returns and individual positions, traders should consider how they are prepared and how they are up-to-date in markets and how they are improving in terms of ongoing training. This regular appraisal will help a trader correct errors, change bad habits and improve overall returns.

Understanding FOMO (Fear of Missing Out)

Traders need to recognize and delete FOMO until it comes into being. While this is not easy, traders should note that there is always another trade and only capital trading they can afford to lose.

Keep a trade journal and make daily reviews

Another perfect way to achieve a good trader's thinking is to maintain a trading journal. Trading newspapers are like daily newspapers – they only have the trades you make. Journals consist of journal entries that can cover everything you believe to be relevant in a particular business.

Standard journal entries include currency pairs, the reasons for entering and exiting a company, and additional market comments. After you close your trade, create the custom to update your journal entry with profit or loss and any other comments that may provide an insight into the company's success.

Making daily reviews will show an abundance of knowledge on your shared patterns of trade that lead to the loss of business. Perhaps most of your pullback businesses became losers? This is demonstrated by your trading journal and helps you develop your business skills.

Observe other successful traders' acts

One of the best ways to learn a skill is to observe the activities of people who have learned it already. Trading does not vary from any other skill and replicating other good traders' methods and work routine will work miracles for your trading attitude.

It might at best be difficult to find a role model for effective traders, but luckily there are plenty of good books that you can choose to get an insight into the thinking of those traders.

Remember that the market owes nothing to you

One common error that many traders constantly make is market overtrading. Particularly after a trade that goes wrong, some traders are pressing for trade opportunities to chase the market just to incur heavy losses by the end of the day.

That's not how the economy works.

The market owes nothing to you, and it might be a good decision every morning to repeat this mantra. There are highly lucrative business arrangements on certain days and none on other days.

This argument relates strongly to the previous topic of emotional management and trading discipline. Don't get mad about the market when a deal becomes a loser – note, there's no feeling about you on the market.

Keep learning

Education is one of the main factors separating good and unsuccessful traders.

Even if you are in the right place, you need a strong business basis to understand the reasons behind such price changes or market reactions. While there are many concepts to learn in trading, it would be your best bet to learn before you find the resources that best fit your needs and trading styles.

Take at least one hour to read a trading book before bedtime to get an insight into other effective traders' activities. Moreover, online trading courses are also an excellent way to increase your business awareness.

Bring an optimistic market attitude every day.

This may seem apparent, but in fact, it is difficult, particularly after successive losses, to maintain a positive attitude while speculating on the forex market. A good outlook will keep the mind free of negative thoughts that appear to interfere with new businesses.

Put your ego aside. Accept that you get the trades wrong and even lose more trades than you win. This may sound like all the bad news, but consistency and diligent risk management also ensure that the average winners are above average cash flows.

Do not trade for trading's sake.

You can only take what you get from the market. Some days you can position fifteen trades and you cannot place a single business for two weeks in other cases. It all depends on what is happening on the market and whether companies appear in the market - which is compatible with your plan.

Bullish and Bearish

Where do these two animal terminologies come from?

The Bull - Indicates the realist market, the origin of the terminology concerns the birth of the " stock exchange " in Flanders in Belgium. Some of these terminologies (very often verses almost always monosyllabic) were used by buyers and their verse resembled the verse of the bull.

The Bear - This expression instead was to indicate in simple terms, the buyers of the market of Alley (*Novel by Daniel Defoe in 1719*) where he directly states that they are a sort of " bear skin sellers ". They are seen as serial speculators, low-end buyers in a time when there was nothing.

Step by Step Instructions to Begin

Options are a foreign term to many traders. They normally appear to new traders as either a source of fear or a gold mine waiting to be mined.

Between these two extremes is where the reality lies.

Options, like all financial items, have a time and place. Fear is a product of a lack of awareness, comprehension, and risk management. Options, when used correctly, may help an investor identify risk, protect their investments, and increase income or returns. However, when used incorrectly or with a high degree of risk, they can easily and fully deplete a portfolio.

It's important to start small, start basic, and start studying when exploring options for the first time.

1. Start small.

It's easy to get overwhelmed by the choices available. Frequently, the percentage change on an option contract would outperform the underlying stock or index by a large margin. For eg, suppose a stock rises 5% and your stock-linked option position rises 20%. Other times, the movement of your option position can be unrelated to the price action of a stock. For example, if a stock rises 5%, but your bullish option falls 20%, you will lose money. This is because, in addition to the underlying stock price, there are other variables that influence the price of an option. Starting small will help you prevent frustration when learning until you grasp these factors.

Emotions play a major role in trading, and not knowing whether you're making or losing money can be incredibly stressful. Greed or anxiety are more likely to emerge, so starting with a lower risk level will help you handle this. Maintaining a small number of different alternative positions can also help you from becoming exhausted or paralyzed by research when you first start out. For the most part, it's a decent strategy for most traders.

2. Start with the basics.

It's probably not a good idea to start your options trading career with an unbalanced skip-strike call butterfly. And, indeed, such a thing does exist.

Combination trades, or those in which several options are used at the same time, can only be undertaken by experts and seasoned traders. Keeping it easy is the best way to secure yourself and your portfolio.

To begin with, do not sell naked options. This means that selling a call or put without an offsetting position would result in a short position. Selling puts (a bullish strategy) becomes more attractive as your experience grows; however, it is unlikely to be a day one trade.

When you first start out, a simple strategy like buying a call (bullish) or selling a put (bearish) should be your target (bearish or protection).

A call is a contract that requires its owner to purchase a given number of shares (usually 100) at a predetermined price (known as the strike price) for a predetermined period of time (the contract's expiration date). The contract's expense is referred to as a premium.

The maximum amount of money a trader will lose is the premium, which is the expense of acquiring the contract. We're defining exactly how much money is at risk in the trade, which I refer to as their defined risk. And, before the expiration date, owning a call gives you infinite upside.

Buying a put is similar to buying a call, except the holder has the option to sell at a predetermined price rather than purchase. It also has a given degree of risk. This strategy can be used if you expect the price of a stock will fall or if you want to protect an established long position. An investor may build a floor under the position for the cost of the put.

It's crucial to differentiate between established risk or "safe" strategies and profitability. When we talk about buying a call or a put, we're talking about a trade that shouldn't get out of hand or ruin your portfolio because you know what you're getting yourself into. For example, if you buy a $100 call on a $100 stock and the stock drops to $20, the most you will lose is $100. Owning the stock might have cost you a lot of money.

On the other hand, if you purchased a $200 put on Gamestop (GME) when the stock was $25 and the stock rose to $400, the loss is limited to $200. Shorting shares at $25, on the other hand, might wipe out your entire portfolio if the stock rises to $400.

Once you have a clear understanding of these concepts, you can move on to more advanced concepts like covered calls, in which you offer a call against an established long position. You agree to sell your stock at a fixed price in return for being paid for selling the call. Note, regardless of what happens with the stock, the premium is yours to hold. Your downside risk is unchanged, with the premium earned reducing it slightly, while the upside is limited to the strike price of the call option sold before the expiration date.

If you sell a call option, make sure you have enough shares to cover the selling of shares if the short call is exercised. In most cases, you'll need 100 shares to sell a call.

3. Begin your studies

It will help you begin studying through a natural course of observation and doing if you start simple and small. You can read all the books you want, but nothing beats seeing a call or seeing something put into effect. Observing how the prices shift when a stock's price and volatility change over time offers you a first-hand look at concepts like delta and implied volatility, as well as time decay, without even realizing it.

It's not a bad idea to read books, watch videos, or read articles about options, but nothing beats a live market and a real trade to illustrate how they work.

Begin little. Simple and wise. Start learning about the simpler, defined-risk approaches to risk management and options trading. Working on a basic understanding by following these simple steps will have you trading options from a comfortable place with an increasing knowledge base before you know it.

Basics of Options Trading and Investing

This chapter is only to introduce the strategies that will then be explored in detail in the dedicated chapter.

Options are conditional derivative contracts that allow contract buyers (option owners) to purchase or sell a security at the selected price. Option buyers are paid by sellers for this right a sum called "premium." If market rates for option holders are unfavorable, they will allow the option to expire without worth, thus ensuring that losses do not exceed the premium. Option sellers (option authors), by comparison, take a higher risk than option buyers and thus need this premium.

Options are divided into options for "call" and "put." Through a telephone call, the buyer acquires the right in the future to buy the underlying asset at a fixed amount, which is called an exercise price or a strike price. With an option, the buyer may gain the right in the future to sell the underlying asset at the default price.

Why trading options instead of a direct asset?

Trading options have certain benefits. The Chicago Board of Options Exchange (CBOE) is the world's largest exchange offering a broad range of stocks, ETFs, and indexes. 1 Trader can create option strategies from purchasing or selling a single option to highly complex ones with multiple simultaneous option positions.

The following are fundamental solutions for beginners.

Buying Calls (Long Call)

This is the favorite strategy for traders who:
are "bullish" or reliable for a specific stock, ETF, or index and want to reduce risk

You want to use leverage to benefit from rising prices
Options are leveraged instruments, i.e., they enable traders to increase the gain by investing smaller sums than would otherwise be needed if the commodity itself was traded. 100 shares of the underlying security are managed by a standard stock option contract.

Suppose a trader wants to invest 5.000 dollars in Apple (AAPL), trading some 165 dollars per share. He or she can buy 30 shares for $4,950 with this number. Suppose that stock prices rise by 10 percent in the next month to $181.50. Unless brokerage, commission, or sales costs are added, the trader's portfolio will be $5,445. The trader will earn a net return on the invested capital of $495, or 10 percent.

Let's just say a call on the stock, which costs $165 and expires approximately one month, costs $5.50 per share, or $550 per deal. Given the investment budget of the trader, he or she can purchase nine options at a cost of $4,950. Since the option contract governs 100 shares, the trader makes an agreement with 900 shares. If stock prices rise 10 percent, the option expires in cash, valuing $16.50 per share (181.50-$165 strike), or $14,850 for 900 shares. This represents a net return on the capital investment of $9,990 or 200 percent, which is a far higher return than direct trade in the underlying asset.

Risk/Reward: The possible loss of a long call from a trader is limited to the premium paid. There is an infinite potential benefit as the pay-off option will rise along with the underlying asset price before its expiry and there is no cap to how big it is potentially.

Buying Put (Long Put)

This is the favorite strategy for traders who:

They are biased on a specific stock, ETF or index, but want to take less risk than a short sales strategy.
You want to use leverage to profit from falling prices
A put option works the same way a call option works, with the added option gaining value as the underlying price decreases. Although short-selling often allows a trader to benefit from falling prices, the risk is limitless with a short position, since there are no limitations on how high a price can rise. If the underlying increases above the strike price of the contract, the option expires literally without value.

Risk/Recompense: possible loss is limited to the premium payable for the options. The overall benefit from the position is reduced as the underlying price cannot drop below nil, while the put option leverages the trader's return, as with a long call option.

Covered Call

This is the favorite place for traders who:

Do not expect any improvement or a small price increase
Want to reduce upside potential in return for insurance against downside?

A covered call strategy includes the purchase of 100 shares of the underlying asset and the sale of a call option. When the trader sells the call, he or she receives the premium from the option, thus reducing the cost base and offering some retroactive security. In exchange, the trader agrees with selling the option to sell the underlying shares at the strike price of the option, thereby limiting its potential.

Assume the merchant purchases 1,000 shares of BP (BP) at $44 per share and writes 10 call options (one per 100 actions contract) concurrently with a strike price of $46 for one month expiring at $0.25 for one share, or $25 for one contract, and a total of $250 for 10 contracts. The $0.25 premium lowers the cost base for the shares to $43.75, which offers minimal downside cover and offers the premium from the option to be compensated from any fall in the underlying to that point.

Where the share price increases over $46, the short call option is exercised (or "call off"), which means that a seller has to supply the stock at the hit price of the option. Here, the trader makes $2.25 for each share ($46 strike price - a cost basis of $43.75).

This example however suggests that the trader does not expect BP to move substantially above 46 dollars or below 44 dollars in the next month. Unless the shares exceed $46 and have been removed before the options expire, the trader will be able to keep the premium clear to free and continue to sell calls to shareholders if he or she wishes.

Risk/Reward: If the stock price increases above the strike price prior to expiry, the short call option may be exercised and the seller is required to sell the underlying shares at an option strike price, even if it is less than the market price. In return for this risk, a protected call strategy offers minimal insurance of the downside in the form of premiums earned when the call option is sold.

Protective Put

This is the favorite strategy for traders who:

Take the underlying asset and want to cover the downside.
A safeguard is a long time, like the strategy we mentioned above, but the goal, as the name implies, is to protect the downside vs to take advantage of a downside move. When a trader owns shares he or she is bullish in the long term but wants to shield him or her from a fall in the short term, he or she may buy a defensive put.
If the price of the basis rises above the fixed price at maturity, the option will expire without value and the merchant will lose the premium, but will still benefit from the rising underlying price. On the other hand, if the price underlying declines, the trader's portfolio loses value, but the loss is mainly related to the benefit from the position of the option. The position can therefore essentially be viewed as an insurance policy.

The trader will lower the strike price to minimize premium payment at the risk of declining insurance against the downside. This can be considered deductible insurance. Suppose, for instance, that an investor acquires 1,000 Coca-Cola (KO) shares in the amount of $44 and wants to protect the investment from adverse price fluctuations over the next two months.

For example, if the trader wishes to protect the investment from falling prices he or she can purchase 10 on-the-money options for a strike price of $44 for $1.23 or $123 for each share, at a total cost of $1.230. If the trader is prepared to accept any downside risk level, though, he or she can choose less expensive out-of-money options like a $40 put. In this scenario, the cost of the option would be much lower at just $200.

Risk/Reward: If the underlying price remains equal or increases, the future liability is limited to the option premium charged as insurance. However, if the price of the underlying decrease is compensated by the rise in the price of the option and is limited to the difference between the original stock price and the price of the strike plus the premium charged for the option. In the example above, the loss is limited to $4.20 per share at the strike price of $40 ($44 - $40 + $0.20).

Other Options Strategies

These strategies may be a little more complicated than just buying calls or orders, but they are structured to help you control the risk of trading options:

Call strategy or buy-in strategies covered: stocks are being purchased and the investor sells call options on the same stock. The number of shares you purchased should be the same as the number of calls you sold.

Married Put Strategy: The investor purchases options for an equal number of shares after purchasing the stock. The married couple operates as a short-term loss insurance policy at a certain strike price. You will also offer the same number of calling options at a higher price.

Protective collar strategy: An investor purchases a cash exchange option while simultaneously developing a cash exchange option for the same stock.

Long Straddle Strategy: The investor simultaneously purchases the call option and a put option. Both options should have the same price and expiry date.

Long Strangle Strategy: Investor buys a cash-out call option and a cash option simultaneously. They have the same expiry date but different strike prices. The price of the strike should be lower than the call strike price.

Types of Options

An option is a derivative, a contract that allows the buyer to purchase or sell the underlying asset at a certain price (expiry date), at a fixed rate, but not the obligation (strike price). Two types of options are available: calls and puts. Options of American style may be exercised at any time before their expiry. Options of European-style can be exercised only on the expiry date.

The buyer has to pay an option fee in order to enter into an option contract. Calls and Puts are the two most common types of options:

1. Call Options

The buyer is entitled to purchase the underlying asset, but not the obligation, at the price set out in the option contract. Investors purchase calls if they expect that the underlying asset price will rise and sell calls if they believe the price will drop.

2. Put options

Puts grant the buyer the right to sell the underlying asset at the strike price stated in the contract, but not the obligation. The author (seller) of the put option must purchase the asset if the put purchaser exercises its right. Investors purchase posts when they expect that the price of the asset will drop and sell posts if they believe that the posts will rise.

Options Payoffs: Calls and Puts

Calls

The purchaser of the call option pays the full option premium at the time the contract is entered into. Then the buyer will benefit if the price moves in his favor. No option will generate additional losses beyond the purchase price. This is one of the most attractive characteristics of purchasing. The buyer ensures limitless profits with known and strictly defined future losses for a limited investment.

If the underlying asset's spot price does not exceed the option strike price until the option expires, the investor loses the money he paid for the option. However, if the price is higher than the strike price of the underlying asset, the call buyer makes a profit. The benefit sum is the difference between the market price and the price of the option, compounded by the incremental value of the underlying asset, minus the value payable for the option.

For example, 100 shares of the underlying stock are stock options. Assume a trader purchases an ABC inventory call option contract for a strike price of $25. He pays 150 dollars for this option. At the expiration date of the option, ABC stock shares sell for $35. The purchaser of the option exercises his right to purchase 100 ABC shares for $25 per share (the hit price of the option). At the current market price, he instantly sells the stock at $35 per share.

For the 100 shares, he paid $2,500 and sold $3,500 ($35 x 100). He earns $1,000 ($3,500 – $2,500) less the $150 fee payable for the option. Therefore, its net profit is $850 ($1,000-$150), minus transaction costs. That's a very good investment return (ROI) for just $150.

Call selling options

The downside of the call option seller is theoretically limitless. If the spot price of the underlying asset exceeds the strike price, the option writer shall therefore incur a loss (equal to the buyer's gain). However, if the underlying asset's market prices do not exceed the option strike price, then the option expires without value. The option seller gains in the value of the commission for the option earned.

Puts

The seller has the right to sell the underlying asset at the price of the option. The profit that the purchaser makes from the option depends on how far below the point price the strike price falls. If the price of the spot is below the strike price, the buyer is "in money." If the spot price remains above the strike price, the option expires untrained. The loss of the option for the purchaser is again limited to the price charged for the option.
The author is "out of the cash" if the spot price for the underlying asset is below the contract's strike price. Their loss is equivalent to the benefit of the option purchaser. If the spot price is higher than the contract price, the option expires unexercised and the writer bags the option premium.

Options Applications: calls and puts

Options: Investors use calls and pick mainly to cover risk in existing assets. For example, it is often the case that an investor who has stocks purchases or sells stock options to hedge his direct investment in the underlying asset. His investment option is intended to compensate at least partially for any losses sustained in the asset. Options can, however, also be used as independent speculative investments.

Hedging – buying puts

If an investor assumes that some stocks in his portfolio will fall in value, but does not want to abandon their position on a long-term basis, they may purchase stock options. If the stock decreases, then the gains in the put options compensate the real stock losses. Investors also apply such a strategy during unpredictable times such as the season of income. They can purchase items on certain stocks or purchase index items to protect their well-diversified portfolio. Mutual fund managers also use puts to minimize the risk exposure of the fund.

Speculation – Buy calls or sell puts

If an investor assumes that a protection price is likely to increase, he may purchase phone calls or sell items to profit from this increase in prices. The overall liability of the investor for purchasing call options is limited to the premium charged for the option. Theoretically, their future benefit is infinite. The extent to which the market price exceeds the optional price and the number of options that the investor owns is calculated.

Things are reversed for the seller of a placed option. Their potential benefit is limited to the premium for the letter. Their potential loss is infinite, proportional to the price on the market below the option strike price when the number of options sold is equal.

Speculation – Selling calls or buying puts

By selling calls or purchasing puts, investors will profit from lower prices. The upside to the call writer is restricted to the premium option. The purchaser is facing a potentially limitless upside but has a small downside equivalent to the price of the option. If the underlying security market price increases, the buyer benefits in the degree to which the market price falls below the optional price. If the hunch of the investor has been incorrect and the rates do not fall, the investor loses only the premium of the option.

Valuing Options

Unlike stock investments, options have to take time and uncertainty into account. That is why it can seem difficult to value premiums for options. Fortunately, it's not as complicated as you may imagine.

The premium of an equity option partially depends on its relationship with the underlying stock. This is demonstrated by the striking price of the option relative to the stock market price at the time of the acquisition of the option. If the option's strike price is the same as the current market price, the option is considered for the money.

A call with a strike price above the market price or an appealing price lower than the market value is considered out of the money. It is out of money because if it expired today it would be worthless

If you buy a Widget Co. $40 call, for example, but it's $37, it's out of cash. If you buy a $115 ComTech stock that is $117, you're also out of the money, as you wouldn't do the same. After all, why do you want to pay $40 for a stock if $37 is available? In contrast, why would you sell an inventory for 115 dollars if people were willing to pay 117 dollars?

You are purchasing an out-of-money option when you think it is over $40 — and in money considering the share fluctuations and the period you are promised before the expiry. This is when the call price is below the current market price or when the put price is higher than the market price. The alternative now has an inherent value — a calculable value.

Obviously, the money options typically have a higher premium than the money options. Yet out-of-the-money options are much faster for the buyer, in percentage terms, than in cash options when the underlying price moves your way. They even worsen more slowly than in the cash options as the underlying stock moves adversely, depending on the period to expire.

Where option premiums were focused exclusively on their inherent value, there would be no need to purchase options other than insurance or hedging. The price for an option will be set. But above the intrinsic value of an option is its external value, the value of the premium is time and uncertainty.

Remember, wasting assets options. You have a set lifetime and die a little before the expiry date is reached. Unlike equity investors, options investors may not have enough time in a sudden reversal to recover losses. This risk can be seen in the premium.

For e.g., say it is January and you want to purchase more options from Widget Co. Actually, the stock is 72 dollars and you don't know when it is going to go up to at least 85 dollars. Ok, you could buy a March call for $85 or a December call for $85. Both are calls on the same stock at the same price, but the prices may still be thousands apart. Why? Why?

An option has no intrinsic value except in cash. The Widget Co. $85 call option needs $13 to be in the money. If you want three months (March) for stocks to increase by $13 or 11 months (December)? Most will choose 11 months and buy a call in December for $85, but it depends on when you expect to switch the price and how much you're willing to pay for additional time.

Options are risky investments and the value is as much a supply and demand slave as anything else you can buy and sell. Furthermore, the more risk that someone can take, the more they want to be paid for it.

With more buyers calling for the same option – and writers need to take more risk – in 11 months something can happen; fewer will happen in three months and you can expect a higher premium on the more-dated option. Please note that the longer the period to expire, the longer the option would have to fulfill your benefit target. This is less risk... and it means a higher premium.

Bear in mind the break-even price when you figure out your profit goal. This is the price that must hit the underlying investment to recover the premium. Based on the price of the underlying share of the instrument, you measure the distance to the break-even price, not the price you paid for that option.

Your purchase, for instance, a Widget Co. March $85 calling option for $5 per share (a $500 premium). The stock will have to rise by $5 (over $85 a share) to recover the premium, so the break-even price is $90 a share. As you have a right to purchase 100 shares of Widget Co. for $85 per share, you will receive $5 per share for a price of $90 or $500 ($5 times 100 shares). This corresponds to the $500 premium you paid to purchase the option. Any more stock price rise is a benefit, $100 for each dollar stock increase.

Do the opposite, for one thing. Divide the premium by 100 and exclude it from the list. When the break-even point has been established, it is time to determine if the risks outweigh the possible benefits.

Differences and Similarities Between Options and Conventional Trading (Options, Stock, Forex)

Forex Trading, also referred to as FX Trading or by many as the foreign currency exchange is a financial market in which an individual can trade domestic currencies to make a profit. Perhaps you feel that the US dollar will become stronger than the British Pound or the Euro. A strategy can be built to manipulate this trade and good profit can be made if the study is right.

Options trading allows you to purchase or sell stock options, futures, etc. for vast quantities that you believe would either go up or down for a certain time. As with Forex Trading, for example, you can use your purchasing power to monitor more stocks or the future than you usually would have. There are, however, variations between Forex and Trading options. Many of the variations are explained below.

24 Hour Trading: Compared to Options Trading, you have a benefit with Forex Currency Trading System (Forex): the ability to trad around the clock, five days a week. The Forex Market is longer available than any other market. If you want to achieve double-digit returns on a sector, it's nice to have unlimited time for these businesses every week. Whenever there is a significant event around the world, you will be one of the first to take advantage of Forex Trading. In the morning, you won't have to wait for a market that you can open if you traded options. You can trade from your machine any hour of the day and night instantly.

Rapid execution of trade:

You get instant trade executions when you use the Forex Currency Trading System. There is no pause, just as can be seen in Options or in other markets. And your order is filled at the best possible price, rather than estimating the price of your order. Your order will definitely not "slip" with choices as it may. In Forex Trading there's far more liquidity than in Options Trading to deal with "slippage."

Liquidity:

The benefit of Forex Trading is that it is more liquid than any other market-like trading options. There is no contrast with the total daily amount in the forex market of nearly two trillion. Foreign currency trading liquidity (Forex) well exceeds that on the options market. This means that when it comes to trading, Forex trades are filled much better than options. This pace brings with it more potential benefits. Couple this with instant trading in Forex Trading, and you can make a lot of trades quick.

No Commissions:

Forex or FX Trading is Commission Free because it's an interbank market that immediately matches buyers with sellers. As in other markets, there are no intermediate brokerage fees. There is a disparity between the bid and the demand price, and Forex trading companies make some profit here. This means that when trading Forex you can save money in contrast with Options Trading where fees occur as you deal with a brokerage company.

Greater use:

Online Forex Trading will provide you with much more leverage than playing options. However, you can also handle putt and call options with Options such that the leverage is significantly increased. Leverage can be really useful if you know what a currency does. In Forex Trades you can reach 200:1 or higher in comparison to less commonly in Options but can be similar. With Forex, there can be considerably more potential benefits if you do the right thing.

Risk is limited and guaranteed:

Since the position limit must be in place for Forex Traders, the risk is reduced since the Forex Trading system's online capabilities automatically trigger a margin call where the margin is greater than the account value in dollars. This stops a Forex Trader from losing too much if it goes the other way. This is a positive protection factor that is not always present in other financial markets. In that with options, you only have a certain time to sell until the options expire, the forex is different from options.

Consider your favorite trading style and the risk you are prepared to tolerate while contemplating the variations between Forex Trading and Options. Forex or FX Trading has some benefits that can benefit you tremendously if you build a good system and remain within your trading limits. When you are ready to go, start researching a good forex company to open a foreign exchange trading account.

What Is the Difference Between Stocks and Options?

Like stocks and future contracts, options are securities subject to binding agreements. The key is that you can buy or sell fundamental security or asset without having to do so, as long as you comply with the rules in the contract for options.

The main differences between stocks and options are:

- Derivatives are options. A derivative is a financial asset that gets value from the underlying security and time rather than its own intrinsic value. For example, IBM stock options are directly affected by IBM stock prices.

- The options have expiry dates, like future contracts, while the stocks do not. In other words, while you can keep an active company's stock for years, at some point in the future an option will end worthlessly. Options are exchanged during the underlying asset trading hours.

- The holder does not have the option to give any part of the underlying security. The right to purchase or sell this security is all about options.

- The major difference between stocks and options is that stocks are ownership shares of the individual companies and options contract with other investors that allow you to bet on the direction in which you feel an equity price is going. But these assets can balance each other in a portfolio, despite their differences.

- One thing to note: finding possible lucrative investments inside a stock or on the market for options may sound exciting, but you might want to explore low-cost index funds and currents before you plunge into the day trading or options trading. These tools combine various assets (such as stocks or bonds) and allow you to diversify your portfolio by making a single investment. Experts also suggest that investors use these funds as the basis of a long-term portfolio—and they can be a strong starting point for start-up investors.

The Stocks

If you are looking for an easy way to start saving more than five years out, like retirement, inventories can be a good option. While there is no guarantee that you will make money — the output of each stock can be unpredictable — the entire US stock market has consistently shown itself to be a solid, long-term investment.

The beauty of investing in stocks is simplicity: you purchase stocks in the expectation that their price will rise to sell at a higher price. That refers to whether you want to keep stocks for years or try to buy and sell stocks actively for short periods such as days or weeks.

For beginner investors and, in particular, people with a long-term plan, the stock is a more popular point of entry into the stock market than options because they are simpler, have lower costs, and a hands-off approach.

After studying stock, you do not have to obsessively review it every day—those you believe have a growth potential that fits your time horizon. You can simply keep an eye on it until the time you need the money or you can warn your online broker if the stock price increases to a level that you want to sell.

The disadvantages of stocks

The stock risk is straightforward: the price would fall and you will lose much or all of your investment. Because each stock's output can be daily unpredictable, experts usually suggest investing in stocks with capital you would not need for at least five years. In order to reduce risk further, it is ideally better to avoid throwing all of your capital into one stock.

Furthermore, how active you can influence success in trade stocks — and how much you pay income taxes on commissions, fees, and capital gains. Committees for stock trading differ, but many online brokers have recently fully removed them, so you can shop around before opening an account. The tax rate on your capital gains depends upon whether you realize a benefit from the selling of your shares, the length of your stock – the rate for investments kept for under one year is higher – and your profits.

Options

Looking for a more tactical investment strategy, smaller investment criteria, and a flexible timing or downside risk approach? You may have options up your alley.

The related investment duration is generally shorter with options, making them more attractive for traders who actively buy and sell. All contracts for options have expiry dates that vary from day to year.

Although many people like the versatility provided by options, namely the time to see how a market takes effect and how a price is locked without a purchasing commitment, they make the investment process more complicated. Instead of making one decision, such as betting that stock prices will increase, you have to make three:

Which way is the stock going?

How high or low is it going to adjust from its current price.

The time frame for this to happen.

This is the easiest option for trading; more complex strategies exist for experienced traders.

Trading options allow you to learn new words like puts, calls and strike rates that might make you assume that these assets are riskier than stocks. This idea may be exaggerated, particularly as investors may allow an option to expire and assume no additional financial liability other than the premium charged and the related trading costs. In addition, long-term investors may use hedging options. For example, the purchase of a put option helps to reduce future losses if the value of your own stock declines.

The disadvantages of options

Trading of options involves a more practical approach than investing in inventory. You will want to use the option before expiry, which means that you have to keep a close eye on the price of the equipment. You can use your online broker to set alarms.

Some options strategies are often riskier than others, so make sure you understand business in advance. Hint: Many experts suggest that regular or weekly options be avoided, which are more suited to more professional traders.

The associated costs, which could be higher than for stocks, are another drawback of the options trade. Options Traders may pay a flat fee per merchandise – usually the same as the stock trading commission of the broker if one is charged – plus a per-contract fee from 15 to 75 cents. The more you deal, the higher your costs – and don't forget, you will even pay selling fees. Finally, as with stocks, ensure that taxes on capital gains are taken into account. You'll be on the hook to pay benefit tax; for the property you have owned for less than a year, these taxes are higher.

Decision making: options vs. stocks

It is entirely a personal decision to decide whether stocks or options are better for you, based on your investment style.

What can be confirmed quite clearly is that, surely, for a beginner who is about to leave, options are highly recommended and not stocks.

Beginners and others who favor convenience typically stick to stocks for their simple design. Many who promote an aggressive approach to investing and want to watch the market will find attractive choices.

But don't believe that you have one commodity to stick to. After all, options traders are inherently inventors if calling options are exercised. Meanwhile, many stock traders use hedging options. Just make sure you understand what you're doing first, whatever you want.

Why and How Options Trading Is Profitable and How Can Generate A Passive Income

The buyer of the call option is profitable if the underlying asset, let's put a stock, is higher than the strike price before it expires. If the price falls under the strike price before expiry, a buyer with a put option makes a profit. The exact benefit level depends on the difference between the share price and the optional price at the end or when the optional position is closed.

If the underlying stock is below the strike price, a caller option writer will make a profit. When the trader writes an option, he gains if the price remains above the strike price. The profitability of an option writer is limited to the premium they earn for writing the option (which is the purchaser's options cost). Writers of options are also known as sellers of options.

Option Buying vs. Writing

If the trade-in options work out, an option holder will make a substantial return on investment. This is because an equity price will go far beyond the strike price.

An option writer returns relatively smaller if the option trading is profitable. This is because the writer just pays the premium, regardless of how far the stock goes. Why, then, write options? And the chances are usually on the choice writer's side. A Chicago Mercantile Exchange (CME) report in the late 1990s found that just over 75 percent of all options for expiry expired without value.

This analysis excludes option positions closed or exercised before expiry. However, for each choice contract at the expiry of the ITM (In The Money), there were three out of cash OTM (Out of The Money) and thus meaningless statistics.

Risk tolerance assessment

This is a quick test to measure your risk tolerance to see whether you are better off as an option buyer or an option editor. Let's assume you can buy or write 10 call option agreements at a price of $0.50 each. Usually, each contract has 100 shares as its underlying asset, with 10 contracts costing $500 ($0.50 x 100 x 10 contracts).

When you purchase 10 call option contracts, you pay the maximum loss of $500. However, technically, the future benefit is unlimited. Then what's the fishing? The possibility of a successful trade is not very high. Although this probability depends on the implicit volatility of the calling option and the time to expire, say 25%.

If you join 10 calling option contracts, on the other hand, the maximum income you earn is $500, while your loss is technically limitless. However, you are very much in favor of the chances of the options exchange, at 75%.

Will you gamble $500 if you know that you are 75% likely to lose your investment and 25% likely to make a profit? Or, would you rather make a maximum of $500, knowing that you are 75% likely to retain the whole or part of the money, but are 25% likely to lose the trade?

The response to the questions gives you an idea of your risk tolerance and whether you are a buyer of options or a writer of options.

It is important to bear in mind that these are general statistics that apply to all options, but at times, being a writer of options or buyer of a particular asset can be more advantageous. Using the right strategy at the right time could dramatically alter these chances.

Risk/reward option strategies

Although calls and calls can be used to shape sophisticated options strategies in different permutations, let us analyze the risks and rewards of the four most fundamental strategies.

Buying a call

This is the most simple strategy choice. This technique is comparatively low since the gross loss is limited to the premium payable for the call, and the maximum premium is theoretically unlimited. But, as previously mentioned, the chances of the trade are usually very poor. 'Low risk' means that the overall option expense constitutes a very small percentage of the resources of the trader. Risking all capital on a single call option would make it an incredibly risky business, as all money could be lost if the option expired without value.

Buying a Put

This is a relatively low-risk approach, but a likely high reward if the company is successful. Purchasing products is a viable option to the riskier short-selling approach of the underlying properties. Puts may also be acquired in a portfolio to cover the downside risk. But because equity indexes usually tend to increase over time, which means stocks on average tend to increase more often than they decrease, the risk/reward profile of the purchaser is marginally lower than that of the purchaser.

Writing a Put

Writing is a preferred tactic for advanced options traders, because the stock is attributable to the put writer in the worst-case scenario (they have to purchase the stock), while the best situation is that the writer keeps all of the premium for the choice. The greatest danger is that the author will end up paying too much for an inventory if it then tanks. The risk/reward profile of put writing is worse than putting or calling as the maximum reward is the recipient's premiums, but the maximum loss is much higher. That said, as previously mentioned, the likelihood of profitability is higher.

Writing a Call

Two types of call writing are accessible, covered, and bare. Another favored technique of moderate to advanced option traders has covered call writing and is usually used to produce incremental income from a portfolio. It includes calling for inventories kept in the portfolio. The only province of risk-tolerant and sophisticated options traders is the uncovered or naked call written, as it has a risk profile close to that of a short sale on stock. The highest reward in telephone calls is the premium paid. The greatest risk of a covered call strategy is to "remove" the underlying inventory. With naked call publishing, the technically infinite maximum loss is just as with short sales.

Options Spreads

Traders or investors also combine options into a spread strategy to purchase one or more options to sell one or more options. Spreading compensates for the premium charged since the premium sold is net against the premium purchased for the options. In addition, the risk and return profiles of a spread limit the possible benefit or loss. Spreads can be produced to benefit from almost any expected price action and vary from basic to complex. As with each choice, any propagation strategy can be purchased or sold.

Reasons to Trade Options

Investors and traders either trad in order to protect open positions (for example, to purchase long-standing items or to purchase calls to protect a short-standing position) or to speculate on possible price shifts of an underlying asset.

The main advantage of using options is leverage. For instance, an investor has $900 to use in a specific company and wants the most. The investor is optimistic about XYZ Inc. in the short term. Thus, suppose XYZ trades at $90. Our investor can purchase up to 10 XYZ shares. However, XYZ also provides three-month calls for $95 for a rate of 3 dollars. Now the investor purchases three call option contracts instead of purchasing the shares. It costs $900 to purchase three call options (three contracts x 100 shares x $3).

Shortly before the call options expire, assume XYZ trades at $103, and the call trades at $8. the investor sells the calls at that point. Here is how each investment return stacks up.

Outright acquisition of $90 XYZ shares: Profit = 13 dollars per share x 10 shares = 130 dollars = 14,4 percent return (130 dollars / 900 dollars).
Three $95 Call Option Contracts purchased: = $8 x 100 x three contracts = $2,400 plus $900 less premium = $1500 = a return of 166.7% ($1,500/$900).
The downside of buying calls instead of shares, of course, is that if XYZ hadn't traded more than $95 by option, calls would have expired without value and all $900 would have gone. XYZ actually had to sell at $98 (95 dollars for the strike price + 3 dollars for payment), which is approximately 9% higher than when the calls had been bought, to break the trade. If the courier's costs are also applied to the calculation in order to be efficient, the inventory can sell much more.

These situations presume that the trader stayed until the end of the contract. This is not important with US choices. The trader could have sold the option to lock a profit at any time before expiry. Or, if it looked as if the stock did not exceed the strike price, it might sell the option for its remaining value to mitigate the loss. For example, if the trader paid $3 for the options, the options could drop to $1 if the inventory price is below the strike price. The trader was able to sell the three contracts for $1, with $300 back from the initial $900, and stop complete losses.

It would also be possible for the investor not to sell them to book profit/losses but to make calls would require the investor to have a large amount of money to purchase the number of shares their contracts reflect. In the above example, this would entail the purchase of 300 shares at $95.

Choosing the right option

Here are some broad guidelines to help you determine which kinds of trade options.

Bullish or bearish

Are you bullish or bearish at the stock, industry, or general market you want to trade? If so, are you rampant, mild, or just boring? This decision will help you determine which choice strategy to use, what cost and expiration to use. Let's presume you're rampantly bullish with the ZYX hypothesis portfolio, a $46 technology stock.

Volatility

Is the market relaxed or volatile? How about ZYX Stock? If the implicated ZYX volatility is not very high (say 20%) it might be a good idea to buy inventory calls, as such calls might be fairly cheap.

Strike Price and Expiration

You should be fine with buying money calls as you are rampantly bullish on ZYX. You don't want to pay more than $0.50 per call option, so you have the choice of going for two months for $49 for $0.50, or 3 months for a strike price of $50 for $0.47. You opt to go to the latter because you feel that the marginally higher price of the strike is more than offset by the additional month.

What if you were only a little optimistic at ZYX, and its implicit 45 percent volatility was three times that of the overall market? In this case, you might consider writing short-term subscriptions to gain premium revenue, instead of purchasing calls as in the previous case.

Option Trading Tips

As an option buyer, you can choose to purchase options as long as possible to allow your trade time to work out. Conversely, if you want to write options, take the shortest possible expiry to minimize your liability.

If you try to balance the above, buying the cheapest options will increase your chances of a successful trade. The implicated volatility of such cheap options is likely to be very poor, and although the chances of effective trade are marginal, the implicated volatility and therefore the option may be below the price. If the exchange works out, then the future benefit will be immense. If the business doesn't work out, buying options with lower implicit volatility could be preferable to buying those with a very high level of implied volatility because of the chance of higher losses (higher premium payments).

A compromise exists between strike rates and the expiry of options, as the previous example showed. An overview of support levels, resistance levels, and main events (for example, the announcement of earnings) is useful in assessing the impact price and expiry date to be used.

Understand the sector of the stock. For example, when clinical trials of a major drug are revealed, biotech stocks frequently trade in binary outcomes. Deep from the money calls or puts, these results can be bought, depending on whether you are bullish or bearish on the stock. Obviously, calling or placing biotech stocks during such events will be extremely risky unless the amount of implied volatility is such high that the premium income gained compensates for this danger. In the same vein, buying deep cash calls or placing low volatility sectors like utilities and telecoms makes no sense.

Use options for trading one-off activities, such as corporate restructuring and spin-offs, and recurrent events such as returns. Inventories can be highly volatile during such cases, which gives the knowledgeable trader of options the chance to cash in. For example, buying cheap money calls before the income report on a stock in a sharp downturn may be a lucrative tactic if it succeeds in meeting reduced expectations and then increases.

Understanding the Purchase and The Trading of Options

Trading stock options can be complex—even more than trading stocks. You determine just how many shares you want when buying a stock, and your broker fills the order at the prevailing. Options trading requires knowledge of advanced techniques, and the options trading process involves a few more steps than opening a standard account.

A four-phase process will allow you to start trading stock options:

1. Open a trading options account

You must show you know what you are doing before you can start trading. (Need to make calls, calls, price strikes, and other lingo trading options?
In contrast with the opening of a stock trading brokerage account, it takes greater capital to open an options trading account. And, since it is difficult to forecast a number of movements, brokers need to know a little more about a potential customer before issuing them a clearance to start trading options.
Brokering companies test potential options traders for their trading expertise, risk awareness, and financial preparation. This information is captured in an Options Trading Agreement used to seek the prospective broker's approval.

You'll have to provide your:
- Investment goals. These generally include revenue, growth, retention of capital or speculation.

- The broker needs to know your knowledge of finance, how long you traded stocks or options, how many trades you make every year, and the scale of your trades.

- Have your liquid net (or investment easily sold for cash), taxable profits, overall net value, and job information on hand.

You want to trade the kinds of choices. Calls, puts, or spreads, for example. And whether they're nude or wrapped. If the option is exercised, the seller or author of options has a duty to deliver the underlying stock. If the author already has the underlying stock, the location of the option is secured. If the location of the option remains unprotected, it is naked.
On the basis of your responses, the broker will normally assign you an initial level of trade based on risk levels (typically 1 to 5, with 1 being the lowest risk and 5 being the highest). This is the key to setting up those types of choices.
Screening can be performed in both directions. The broker with which you want to trade is your most significant investor. It is particularly important for investors who are new to options trading to find the broker that offers the tools, analysis, advice, and support they need.

2. Choose which options to buy or sale

As a refresher, a call option is a contract which grants you a right, but not an obligation, to purchase stock within a certain time at a default price (called the strike price). A put option gives you the right to sell the shares before the contract ends, but not the obligation.

Depending on the direction in which you expect the underlying stock to shift to decide which options to take:

- If you believe the stock price will rise: buy a call option, sell a put option

- If you think the stock price remains stable, sell a call or sell a put option

- If the stock price falls: purchase a position option, sell a call option.

3. Predict the price of the option

When an option is purchased, it only stays valuable if the inventory price closes 'money' for the expiry duration of the option. You'll want to purchase an option with a striking price that represents where you predict the stock is over the lifespan of the option. (For call options, it is above the strike; for put options, it is below the strike.)

For example, if you assume that a company's share price of 100 dollars will reach 120 dollars on some future date, you might buy a call option for a strike price below 120 dollars (ideally, a strike price no more than 120 $ less the option cost, so that this option stays profitable for 120 dollars). If the stock is actually higher than the strike price, your option is the money.

Similarly, if you agree that the share price of the Company is going to drop to 80 dollars, you'll buy a set fee with a strike price above 80 dollars (ideally a strike fee no lower than 80 dollars plus the fee of the fee so you have the opportunity to continue profitable at 80 dollars). If your stock falls below the strike price, the money is your option.

Only no strike price can be selected. Option quotes called an option chain or matrix, including a number of strike prices available. The increases between strike rates are industry-level — e.g., $1, $2,50, $5, $10 — and are stock-based.

The price that you pay for an option known as the premium has two components: the inherent value and the value of time. If the stock price is higher than the strike price, the value is the difference between the strike price and the share price. Time is whatever remains and affects, among other elements, the volatility of the stock, time of expiry, and interest rates. For example, if you have a calling option of $100, the inventory costs $110. Let's say the premium of the option is $15. The intrinsic value is 10 dollars (110 dollars minus 100 dollars), the time value of 5 dollars.

This brings us to the last decision you must make before you purchase a contract with options.

4. Determine the option time frame

The expiration date of each option contract is the last day that you can exercise the option. You can't pull a date out of thin air here, either. When you call an option chain, your options are limited to those offered.

There are two types of options, American and European, which rely on the exercise of the options contract. American option holders may exercise at any point up to the expiry day, while European options holders may exercise on the expiry day only. As American options give the option buyer more choice (and a higher risk for the option seller), they typically cost more than their European counterparts.

Dates of the expiry can vary from days to months to years. Daily and weekly choices are usually the riskiest and reserved for experienced traders in options. Monthly and annual expiry dates are preferable for long-term investors. Longer expirations allow the stock more time to travel and time to complete its investment thesis. The longer the expiry date, the more costly the option is.

A longer-term is also useful because, if the stock trades are below the strike price, a time value may be retained. When the expiration approaches the time value of the option declines and investors do not want to see their purchased options fall, possibly expiring worthless if the stock ends below the cost of the strike. When a trade is opposed to them, they normally still can sell some remaining time value—and this is more likely if the option contract is longer.

Understanding the Options Trading Mechanism

Options were initially traded in the OTC (Over The Counter) market where contract terms were negotiated. The OTC market's benefit over exchanges is that option contracts can be tailor-made to suit the needs of the option buyer: price strikes, expiration dates, number of shares. Transaction costs are however higher and liquidity is lower. Trading options really started when the first listed exchange of options — the Chicago Board of Options Exchange (CBOE)— was organized in 1973 for trading structured agreements, dramatically expanding the demand and liquidity of options. The CBOE was the original options exchange but by 2003 it had been replaced by the New York-based electronic International Securities Exchange (ISE). Most of the options offered in Europe are electronically traded.

Types, Position Variations, and Typical Assets

The buyer of an option has the right to exercise the option, but not the responsibility. The maximum loss for the purchaser is the premium charged for the option. Note that the premiums are paid by a trader to secure the right, at a certain amount, to purchase or sell an underlying asset. On the other hand, the potentially limitless future benefits. However, the seller (writer) is limited to the maximum benefit after writing the option. There is no limit to the possible loss.

Some of the symbols used to represent relevant options include:

X = strike price
S_t = Price of the underlying asset at time t
C_t = the market value of a call at time t
P_t = the market value of put option at time t
t = the time to maturity/expiration of the option

Call Options

The owner/holder/buyer has the right to purchase the underlying stock at the expired price but not at the expired price. The buyer is said to be long in the deal, while the seller is said to be short.

The buyer cannot exercise the option if the stock price is less than or equal to the stock price at maturity because the payoff is zero. If the stock price is higher at maturity than the exercise price, the option will most likely be exercised. The payout is proportional to the difference between the market price and the strike price $(S_t - X)$.

Put Options

The holder/customer has the right, but not the responsibility, to sell the underlying stock at a fixed price. At the end of the contract, the buyer can only benefit if the current market price is lower than the exercise/strike price. The wage is equivalent to $(X - S_t)$ If the stock is X or higher, the payoff is zero.

Types of Options

Options that can be exercised at any time, before or before the expiry period are known as American options. Those that can be exercised only on the expiry/maturity date are known as European options. The most exchange-traded options are American, while most traded options are European options on counter markets. Because they are only tradeable in maturity, the Black-Scholes-Merton model can easily evaluate European options. Numerical procedures, such as binomial trees, are used to evaluate US choices. The date of exercise is the date stated in the contract on which the contract matures (maturity date). The fixed price of the commodity to be sold for the future is known as the exercise price (or the strike price).

Moneyness of options

Suppose options should be exercised today. The alternative is to say:
- If it gives a positive payoff, in cash, if it provides a negative payoff, and in cash if it is zero.

- A call (position) option is said to be in the money if, at maturity of the contract, the strike price is lower (higher) than the asset price. If the striker's price at the maturity of the contract is higher (less) than the asset price, a call-out option is said to be out of the money. If the asset price is equal to the strike price at maturity, an option is said to be for money.

Example of the Moneyness of options

A graph is a perfect way to visualize this idea. We have an AAPL call option for a strike price of USD 150. Whenever the underlying price (AAPL stock) is higher than USD, the choice is money:

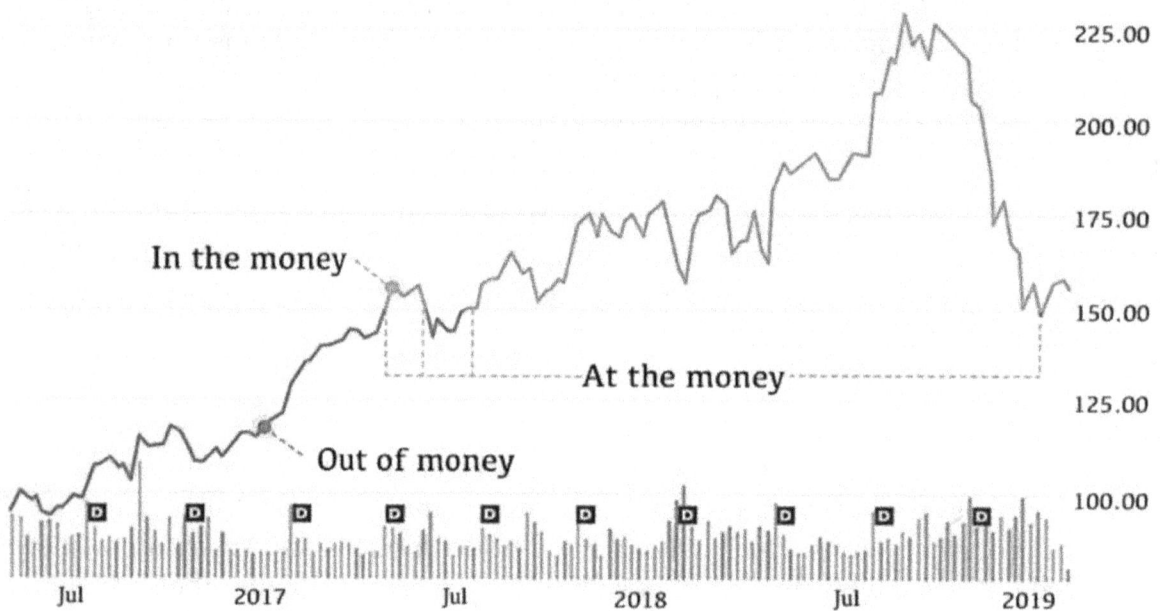

Note that with a USD 150 strike option, the exact opposite would be true – the option is out of money at every moment the underlying stock is more than USD 150.

Call Options Income

Example 1: European calling P&L
Assume that a trader buys a $50 strike price for an asset currently trading at $40 out of the cash European call option. The choice is valid for 6 months and has a premium of $5. What are the profits/losses of the trader if the price of the commodity is I 40 and (ii) 60 dollars?

For an existing asset price of $40

- This option is not exercised.

- Therefore, the trader incurred a $5 loss, the premium charged for the option.

- The call seller makes a profit of $5.

For an existing $60 asset price

- This option is exercised.

- The trader buys the assets at 50 dollars and then sells them at 60 dollars.

- As a result, the trader is going to earn $60 (current asset price) - $50 (strike price) – $5 (premium payable) = $5

- The seller would be affected by a loss of $5.

Net Loss on Call Options

Often, by using an option, a trader can get a net loss. The present price of the underlying asset varies from the strike price to the strike price plus the premium paid. In this example, when the current price is between $50 and $(50+5) = $55, the trader will incur a net loss.

Example 2: Net Loss on European calls
Suppose the current asset market price in Example 1 is $53. What is the net loss of the trader?
If the trader wishes not to exercise the option, he loses $5.
If the option is exercised the trader has a negative benefit: 53 dollars – 50 dollars – 5 dollars – 2 dollars.
Although the trader takes a loss by exercising the option, the loss is lower than the loss if the option is not exercised. In such a case, the gains made by the seller of the call option are also under $5.

Profits on Put Options

Example 3: European Putting P&L
Assume that a trader buys a $50 strike price from the European money for a commodity that is currently selling at $40. The choice is valid for 6 months and has a premium of $5. What are the earnings of the trader if the price for the underlying asset is I $40 and (ii) $60 at maturity?

For an existing asset price of $40

This option is exercised.
- The trader profit would be 10 dollars less the premium of 5 dollars.

- Since it's a zero-sum game, the seller would lose five dollars.

For an existing asset price of $60

- The choice will not be used

- The buyer will forfeit the $5 bonus, and the seller will receive the $5 fee charged in advance.

Net Loss on Put Options

If the actual market price of this asset is between the hit price minus the price charged and the hit price, in this case between $45 and $50, the trader will incur a net loss. For e.g., if the underlying price expires at $49, the buyer will make 1 dollar of money from the option and will lose 5 dollars of the upstream premium, for a net loss of 4 dollars. It's even better than missing the entire $5 premium option!

Payoffs

Denoting the price of the asset at maturity as S_t and the strike price as X, the payoffs from option positions are as shown below.

Long Call: $\max (S_t - X, 0)$
Short Call: $-\max (S_t - X, 0) = \min (X - S_t, 0)$
Long Put: $\max (X - S_t, 0)$
Short Put: $-\max (X - S_t, 0) = \min (S_t - X, 0)$

Intrinsic Value and Time Value

The intrinsic value is the value of the option if the option were to be exercised immediately. It is the same mathematical formula as if the payoff of the option was today.

Long Call: $\max (S_t - X, 0)$
Long Put: $\max (X - S_t, 0)$

The time value of an option is the difference between the option premium and the intrinsic value:

Option premium = Time value + Intrinsic value

Exchange-Traded Options on Stocks

Options traded in exchanges are American-style options. The largest exchange in the world is the Chicago Board Options Exchange (CBOE). Traders with a short position are randomly allocated (assigned) traders with a long position. A single option contract is the right to trade 100 shares.

Maturity of Stock Options

The CBOE has three cycles of trade (maturity dates):
- Jan Cycle: January, April, July, October

- Feb Cycle: February, May, August, November

- March Cycle: March, June, September, December

The CBOE equally offers weekly options (short-term options) and LEAPS (Long Term Equity Anticipation Securities). LEAPS are simply publicly traded options contracts with expiration dates that are longer than one year.

Strike Prices

The CBOE sets strike rates in various ways.
Three values closest to the current price of an underlying asset are the striking prices of a subordinate asset.

Example: Quoted Strike prices
Suppose the underlying asset's price is $20. The striking prices of the asset listed will be the three closest prices multiples of 2.5 to the current price. It'd be $17.5, $20, and $22.5 in this situation.
If the value of the asset is below $17.5, trading options start with a strike price of $15. On the contrary, if the prices of the commodity exceed $22,5, trading options with a price of $25 will begin. These rules ensure that many opportunities for trade are open.
Same style options form a class. Class options with a particular maturity and strike pricing form an option sequence.

The effect of dividends and stock splits

Dividends in Stock

The stock dividend includes issuing additional shares to the shareholders instead of paying cash. For instance, if a company declares a stock dividend of 2 percent, the shareholders will receive two additional shares for every 100 shares owned.
Cash-dividends are not normally modified for currency-traded options. In other words, no changes are made to the terms of the option contract when a cash dividend happens.

Stock splits

A shares division includes the total number of outstanding shares by issuing more shares at a prescribed ratio to shareholders. For instance, a 2-for-1 share sharing means that one shareholder is awarded one more share for any two shares owned.

If a stock has a split b-for-a-share, the share price decreases by (a/b). This is, however, a theoretical assertion. In reality, the share price after division can be different. The number of shares would increase by many (b/a) shares.

The terms of the contracts of exchange-traded options are adapted to represent anticipated market price adjustments resulting from a stock split.

Non-standard Products

They include

Flexible exchange (FLEX) option: These are stock exchange options, so there is far more flexibility. The price and expiry dates of the strike can be changed if the parties so wish.

ETF options: these are options of the US-style which are resolved by offering the underlying shares instead of cash.

Weekly options: Short-term options with a maturity of about 7 days. It is produced on a Thursday, and the deadline is Friday of the following week.

Binary options: Binary options have a fixed payout if ITM (In The Money) is expired.

Binary Credit Event Options (CEBOS): The payout for CEBOs is triggered if the reference entity suffers from a credit event prior to the expiry of the option.

Deep Out-of-The-Money (DOOM) options: They are built for ITM only if the price of the underlying asset is significantly decreasing.

Trading commissions, market makers, closing, and margin requirements

Most exchanges of options use market makers to make trading easier. The retail manufacturer quotes deals and costs.

A commission relates to the fee that a broker charges for his efforts to facilitate a deal. The costs of the Commission depend on the scale of the exchange and on the type of broker involved. They minimize the returns of the investor.

Options can be locked, as can potential markets, by taking an offsetting role.

In order to discourage investors from influencing only the options markets, the CBOE sets a position and limits on options traded:

The role limit refers to the amount of contracts that an investor may enter into on the same market side. Medium calls and short calls are on the one side of the market while short calls and long calls are on the other.

The cap is the number of contracts to be exercised in five working days.

The word 'margin' refers to the collateral that the option writer places as a way to ensure that they comply with their contractual obligations in the options trading. The margin requirements vary between brokers and depend on the nature of the asset. Options maturing before 9 months cannot generally be purchased on a margin. Those that expire after 9 months may be bought up to 25% of the purchase price through borrowing.

Warrants, convertibles, and employees stock options

Warrants are calling options provided by a corporation.

Convertible bonds are bonds that can be exchanged into equities using a pre-determined ratio.

Employee stock options are issued to its employees by a corporation.

When the holder of the three securities above exercises his right to buy stock in the company, the company issues further shares.

Differences and Similarities Between Day Trading and Swing Trading

The time period for traders to choose trade can have a huge effect on their trading strategy and profitability. Day traders open several positions and close them within a single day. In comparison, swing traders trade for several days, weeks, or even months. These two different types of trading will accommodate different traders, depending on the amount of available resources, time available, psychology, and the market being traded.

One trade style is no better than another and it just comes down to the style that fits the circumstances of the particular trader. Some traders want to do one thing or the other, while others may be day traders, swing traders, and investors all at the same time.

Day Trading VS Swing Trading: Possible returns

Day trading attracts traders who want fast return compounds. Assume that a trader is at risk of 0.5% (half) of its resources for each exchange. If you lose, you will lose 0.5%, but if you win, you will lose 1% (2:1 reward-to-risk ratio).

Suppose, too, that they win half of their trades. If you do six trades a day — an average — you will add about 1.5 percent to your balance every day, lower trading fees, and even 1 percent a day, the trader's account will grow unmatched by over 200 percent over the year.

On the other side, while the numbers appear to be easy to duplicate, nothing is ever so easy. Having winners double the losers, thus earning 50% of all trades you take, doesn't come easily. You can make fast profits, but your trading account also can be depleted quickly by daily trading.

Swing trading is slower than day trading, but some swing trades can still lead to large profits or losses quickly. Suppose a swing trader follows the same risk management rule and risks 50% of its resources on every trading in order to try to make 1% to 2% of his profits.

Assume you are earning 1.5% on average on winning businesses, losing 0.5% on losing businesses. Six trades are made each month and half of the trades are won. In a typical month, the Swing Trader could account for 3 percent, indicating lower fees. Over the year, this is approximately 36 percent that sounds fantastic but provides less potential than the potential earnings of a day trader.

These examples show the disparity between the two trading types. If the amount of trade won is altered, the average benefit in contrast with the average loss or the number of trades will significantly impact the profit potential of a strategy.

In general, day trading has more potential for benefit, at least in smaller accounts. If the account size increases, it becomes harder for all resources to be used successfully in very short-term businesses.

The more money they have day traders will see their percentage returns decrease. Their dollar returns may also rise, as 5 percent of one million dollars is well over 20 percent of 100,000 dollars. Swing traders are less likely to do this.

Varying requirements for capital

The criteria for capital differ according to the industry. Day trading and swing traders can begin with different capital amounts depending on the trading on the stock, forex, or future market.

Day trading stocks in the United States need at least $25,000 in accounts balance.

There is no legal minimum for swinging trade stocks. However, a swing trader would probably want at least $10,000 on his account, and preferably $20,000 if he wishes to gain revenue.

There is no legal minimum for day trading on the market, but traders are advised to start with at least $500, but preferably $1,000 or more. The minimum recommended for swinging trade is around $1,500, but ideally more. This amount of money allows you to join at least a couple of companies at a time.

Start with at least $5,000 to $7,500 for day trading futures and even better more cash. These quantities depend on the trading of the future contract. Day trading can require much more money in some contracts and may require fewer contracts, such as micro contracts.

You need at least $10,000 and perhaps $20,000 or more to swing trade in a wide range of potential contracts. The amount required depends on the particular contract margin conditions being traded.

Trading Times Differ

Trading on both days and swing requires time, but day trading usually takes a lot longer. Day traders normally trade for a minimum of two hours a day. To add to the time for the planning and the chart/trading analysis, at least three to four hours will be spent on the machine. If a trader chooses to trade more than a few hours a day, the time spent increases significantly and becomes a full-time job.

On the other hand, swing trading will take far less time. For example, if you swing off a regular map, new trades can be found and orders can be updated in about 45 minutes a night. These tasks might not even be necessary at night.

Some swing traders who do business over the last week or months will just have to search for shops and change orders once a week to get the time commitment down to around an hour a week rather than a night, or even to update the orders at night.

Day trading is often necessary when a market is open and active. The most successful day-trading times are limited to certain times of the day. If during those hours you can't trade daytime, then choose swing trading as a better choice. Swing traders may search for shops or position orders, even when the market is closed, at any time of day.

Swing traders are less influenced by fluctuations in asset prices second to second. They concentrate on the bigger picture, normally looking at regular charts, which makes putting business perfect when the market closes on a certain day. Day traders make money from second-by-second movements so that they have to participate as the action takes place.

Concentration, time, and practice

Swing and day trading takes both a lot of effort and experience to reliably produce profits. However, the requisite information is not inherently "book smarts." Successful trade benefits from discovering a strategy that creates a boom or a profit over a large number of trades, and then continually implementing this strategy.

Some business experience and a profitable approach will begin to generate income with a lot of practice. Every day, rates change differently from the last day. This fluctuation means that the trader must be able to execute its strategy under different situations and adjust as conditions change.

This versatility requirement poses a challenging challenge. Consistent findings come only from the implementation of a plan under tons of different business scenarios. That takes time and should include hundreds of businesses in a demo account before they risk real money.

Day trading or swing trading is also a personality preference. Day trading usually entails more work, requires long-term concentration and unbelievable discipline. People who like action, quick reflexes, or like video games and poker appear to become traders on the day.

Swing exchange occurs at a slower rate with even longer delays between acts as the entry or exit of transactions. It also needs high tension and tremendous discipline and patience.

It does not take as much continuous attention, so swing trading might be the better choice if you have trouble keeping focused. Fast reflexes do not matter in swing trading, because trading will take place after market closures and prices stop moving.

Day trade and swing trade give both freedoms in the sense that a trader is their boss. Traders are typically self-employed. They finance their accounts and are responsible for all losses and income generated. Swing traders can be argued for more flexibility as swing trading takes less time than day trading.

The Last Comparison

Each style of trading is not better than the other; it meets different needs. Day trading has more benefit opportunities in smaller trading accounts, at least in percentage terms. Swing traders have a greater chance to keep their percentage returns up to a limit, even as their account increases.

Capital requirements vary considerably across the various markets and types of exchange. Day trading takes longer than swing trading, while both take a lot of practice to be consistent. Day trading is the only option for lovers of action. Those who seek a less stressful and less time-consuming alternative will swing.

What are Greeks (Delta, Gamma, Vega, Theta) / Monitoring Options Greek Changes

Trying to predict the price of a single option or place with many options, as adjustments to the market can be hard work. As the price of the option does not always seem to shift with the price of the underlying asset, it is important to consider the factors that affect the movement in an option's price and its effect.

Options traders also refer to the positions of Delta, Gamma, Vega, and Theta. These terms are known collectively as Greeks and provide a method to assess the sensitivity of the price of an option to quantifiable factors. The words can seem confusing and overwhelming to new options traders, but the Greeks refer to basic concepts which help you to better understand the risk and prospect of an option.

Check for Greek values

First of all, the numbers given are purely theoretical for each of the Greeks. This means that the values are predicted using mathematical models. The majority of information you need on trade options — for example, the offer, requests and last rates, amount, and open interest — is factual information from the different exchanges of options and distributed by your data services and/or brokering company.

The Greeks must be measured and their precision is just as good as the model used for their estimation. You need access to a computerized solution to measure it for you. This knowledge is also provided by most retail brokerages (interactive brokers). Naturally, you can learn math and measure Greeks by hand for each option, but this would be impractical considering the many available choices and timescales.

Below is a matrix showing various options for stock currently trading at $60 in March, April, and May 2018. The mid-market price, Delta, Gamma, Vega, and Theta for each alternative are formatted. When we talk about what every Greek means, you can refer to this example to help you understand the concepts.

	CALLS				DESCRIPTION		PUTS			
MID	DELTA	GAMMA	VEGA	THETA	STRIKE	MID	DELTA	GAMMA	VEGA	THETA
					MAR 16'18 (4 DAYS)					IV: 60.5%
25.10	1.000	0.000	0.000	0.000	35		0.000	0.000	0.000	0.000
20.10	1.000	0.000	0.000	0.000	40		0.000	0.000	0.000	0.000
15.10	1.000	0.000	0.000	0.000	45		0.000	0.000	0.000	0.000
10.12	0.994	0.004	0.001	-0.010	50	0.01	-0.006	0.004	0.001	-0.010
5.30	0.919	0.038	0.010	-0.075	55	0.20	-0.081	0.038	0.010	-0.073
1.69	0.523	0.105	0.025	-0.192	60	1.58	-0.477	0.105	0.025	-0.189
0.36	0.145	0.053	0.014	-0.122	65	5.28	-0.856	0.053	0.014	-0.120
0.11	0.042	0.017	0.006	-0.058	70	10.00	-0.959	0.017	0.006	-0.055
0.06	0.005	0.003	0.001	-0.009	75	14.95	-0.996	0.003	0.001	-0.004
					APR 20'18 (39 DAYS)					IV: 54.7%
25.23	0.997	0.001	0.002	-0.003	35	0.04	-0.003	0.001	0.002	-0.002
20.30	0.984	0.003	0.007	-0.008	40	0.09	-0.016	0.003	0.007	-0.006
15.48	0.951	0.009	0.021	-0.017	45	0.27	-0.049	0.009	0.021	-0.015
11.05	0.870	0.020	0.038	-0.032	50	0.81	-0.130	0.020	0.038	-0.030
7.28	0.725	0.031	0.065	-0.048	55	2.03	-0.275	0.031	0.065	-0.046
4.45	0.543	0.037	0.077	-0.057	60	4.20	-0.458	0.038	0.077	-0.054
2.55	0.368	0.035	0.071	-0.054	65	7.30	-0.638	0.035	0.071	-0.052
1.42	0.233	0.028	0.056	-0.045	70	11.15	-0.769	0.028	0.056	-0.042
0.80	0.143	0.020	0.048	-0.034	75	15.57	-0.860	0.020	0.047	-0.031
					MAY 18'18 (67 DAYS)					IV: 60.5%
25.30	0.990	0.002	0.008	-0.005	35	0.06	-0.010	0.002	0.008	-0.003
20.48	0.970	0.005	0.019	-0.009	40	0.19	-0.030	0.005	0.019	-0.007
15.88	0.922	0.011	0.037	-0.017	45	0.55	-0.079	0.011	0.037	-0.015
11.68	0.833	0.019	0.061	-0.027	50	1.33	-0.168	0.019	0.061	-0.024
8.15	0.703	0.027	0.085	-0.036	55	2.77	-0.298	0.027	0.086	-0.033
5.38	0.551	0.031	0.101	-0.040	60	5.00	-0.450	0.031	0.101	-0.037
3.40	0.404	0.030	0.102	-0.039	65	8.03	-0.598	0.030	0.101	-0.036
2.10	0.282	0.026	0.087	-0.034	70	11.75	-0.721	0.026	0.086	-0.031
1.29	0.191	0.020	0.077	-0.028	75	15.93	-0.814	0.021	0.075	-0.025

The left part of the call displays the call options and the right part shows the put options. Notice that the strike prices in the middle are blue vertically. The options are those with strike prices above 60 for calling and strike prices below 60 for calling. The options for money have a 60 and lower strike price for calls and 60 and higher for calls (the column is highlighted in blue). The expiration dates increase from March to April and then to May as you pass from top to bottom. The actual number of days left before expiry is shown in parentheses in the center of the matrix definition column.

The above statistics for Delta, Gamma, Vega, and Theta are normalized for dollars. To normalize Greek dollars, simply multiply them by the option's contract multiplier. For most stock options, the contract multiplier will be 100 (shares). How the various Greeks switch under different circumstances depends on how far the strike price from the current stock price is and how much time remains before the end of the stock.

As the price changes underlying stock—Delta and Gamma

Delta tests the sensitivity of the potential value of the option to a price shift for the underlying asset. It is usually interpreted as a minus 1 number which shows how much the value of an option can change when the price of the underlying stock increases by a dollar. As an alternate convention, the Delta may also display the total dollar sensitivity of the value 1, which includes 100 shares of the underlying option, as a value between -100 and +100. The standard Deltas above display the actual sum of the dollar you are gaining or losing. For e.g., if you owned a Delta of -45.2 on December 60, you could lose 45,20 dollars if the inventory price rises by a dollar.

Call options have positive deltas and negative deltas have options. Options for money normally include deltas of about 50. Deep-in-the-money options can have an 80 or higher Delta, while deep-in-the-money options are 20 or less. As inventory prices adjust, Delta changes as the option get even higher in or out of money. When a stock option gets really far into the money (nearly 100 dollars), it starts trading like a stock by shifting almost the dollar by the stock price. Meanwhile, far-out options in absolute terms of the dollar would not change much. Delta is also a very significant number when building combined positions.

As Delta is such a significant factor, options traders want to know how Delta will adjust with changing stock prices. For every one-point increase of the underlying asset, Gamma calculates the rate of change in Delta. It is a useful method to help you predict shifts in an option's Delta or an overall role. Gamma will be bigger for money options and will be smaller for in- and out-of-the-money options. Unlike Delta, for both calls and puts, Gamma is always optimistic.

Volatility changes and the passage of time—Theta and Vega

Theta is a measure of an option's decay of time, the dollar sums an option loses every day because of the passing of time. Theta rises as an option hits the expiry date for the money options. Theta decreases as an option reaches expiry with in and out-of-the-money options.

Theta is one of the most relevant principles for a trader of initial options to consider as it describes the effects of time on the premium of bought or sold options. The longer you go, the smaller the time decline would be an option. If you want an alternative, buying long-term contracts is beneficial. If you want a plan that benefits from time decline, you want to shorten the short-term possibilities, so that the value loss occurs rapidly due to time.

The last Greek we're going to look at is Vega. Vega and volatility are misunderstood by many. Volatility tests volatility in the asset. Vega tests the price sensitivity of an option for volatility adjustments. A change in volatility affects and equals all calls. The rise in volatility will increase the prices of all asset options, and the reduction in volatility will result in a fall in value for all options.

However, each option has its own Vega and will respond differently to changes in volatility. The effect of shifts in volatility is higher for the options of money than for the options of input or out of money. Although Vega affects and positions calls in a similar way, it seems to affect calls more than calls. Perhaps because of demand growth expectations over time, this impact is more pronounced in long-term options such as LEAPS.

To understand combined trade with the Greeks

You may also use the Greeks on individual options for positions combining many options. This will help you calculate, no matter how nuanced, the different risks of each trade you consider. Given the variety of risk exposures to optional positions and the risks are significantly different over time and with market fluctuations, it is crucial that they are understood easily.

Below is a danger diagram showing the likely gain/loss of a spread of vertical call debit combining 10 long May 60 calls with 10 short May 65. The horizontal axis shows upward XYZ Stock prices left to right, while the vertical axis shows profit/loss. Today, the stock is trading at $60.22.

Quote Details

Bid/Ask	1.79 x 1.84
Size	78 x 22

Performance

Return/Risk	1.77
Profit Probability	37%
Max Return (18% chance)	3,195 / 174%
Max Loss (49% chance)	1,805 / 100%
Aggressiveness	Unknown
MinInvest	1,826
Break Even	61.81
Commission	26
Commission%	1
Mgn Imp	0

Performance Graph

P&L ▼ — Mar13 (66 days) •• May16 '18 ▼

Scenarios

10.0% Move ▼ May16 '18 ▼

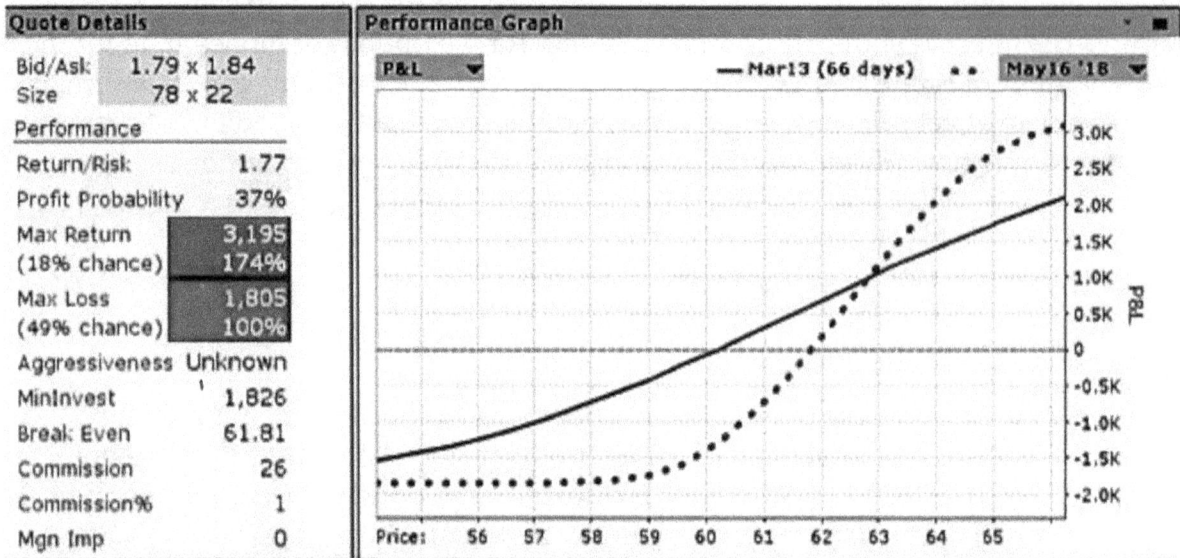

	-10%	-5%	-1%	Current	+1%	+5%	+10%
Underlying	54.20	57.21	59.62	60.22	60.83	63.24	66.25
P&L	-1840.00	-1838.62	-1567.15	-1280.05	-864.23	1378.58	3081.82
Delta	0.00	0.04	3.70	5.89	7.81	9.41	1.33
Gamma	0.00	0.12	3.51	3.59	2.69	-1.00	-1.87
Vega	0.00	0.01	0.21	0.21	0.17	-0.07	-0.13
Theta	0.00	-0.01	-0.69	-0.73	-0.57	0.21	0.44

The dotted line shows the spreading location PNL through May along with the solid line that shows the current PNL. This is obviously a bullish position (in reality it is sometimes called a spread of bull calls) and would only be put if you expected the stock to increase the price.

The Greeks demonstrate how vulnerable it is to stock price, fluctuations, and time shifts. The scenario segment of the underlying stock has a 10 percent move. The table above shows what profit/loss, Delta, Gamma, Vega, and Theta are expected to be in place on 16 May 2018. It might seem complicated, but you can follow Investopedia's options for beginners if you want to learn basic ways of thinking about Greco. These principles are easily digestible.

Minor Greeks

Besides the above risk factors, options traders can also look at derivatives of second and third-order which imply changes in these risk factors as changes in other variables occur. While less widely used, they are still useful to gain a thorough grasp of the entire risk profile of an option position.

The Lambda, Epsilon, Vomma, Vera, Pace, Zomma, Color and the Ultima are some of them.

These Greeks are influencing things like the delta shift with a change in volatility etc. Though less well-known, they are increasingly used in trading options, since computer software can easily calculate the complex and often esoteric risk factors.

The Greeks help to calculate the risks and potential benefits of a choice. You will begin to apply this to your existing techniques once you have a good understanding of the basics. It is not sufficient simply to know the overall risk capital in an optional role. In order to understand the likelihood of a company making profits, a number of risk-exposure metrics must be calculated.

As the circumstances are changing constantly, Greece offers traders a way of assessing how susceptible a particular trade is to price fluctuations, uncertainty fluctuations, and time span. Combining a Greek understanding with the powerful insights offered by risk graphs will take your options trading to a different stage.

Technical and Sectors Analysis

Options, unlike traditional assets and financial instruments, offer investors and traders more versatility in terms of taking advantage of market dynamics, seasonal trends, volatility disparity, and other factors. When it comes to making investment and trading decisions, investors and options traders rely heavily on technical analysis. Most option traders and investors foresee the three forms of price action and buy or sell calls and put accordingly. The three price movement options that traders are looking for are as follows:

Strong Movement in One Direction

The simplest strategy for locating candidates that are moving rapidly is to use a 20-day exponential moving average. As compared to the standard moving average, the exponential moving average is even more receptive because it gives more weight to the most recent price. As a result, it's a great tool for traders to use to assess the strength of a pattern.

The 90-day market highs are another valuable method for technical analysis in options trading. Financial assets that hit their 90-day highs are likely to continue heading in the same direction with increased momentum, according to several backtests. Many traders conclude that stocks and other financial assets are overpriced when they sell over their 90-day price high, but most big price breakouts that last several weeks all begin with a break of the 90-day price high.

Mild Directional Movement

This type of price change usually occurs as a result of a pullback, a rebound, or a continuation of momentum following a pause. This price change normally happens during an ongoing trend, when the market pauses and re-balances before moving in the direction of the main trend.

Identifying assets that are pulling back during a powerful upwards trend is a simple and efficient way to spot mild directional momentum in options. The Relative Strength Index is a useful metric for this type of analysis. Although there are many oscillators that are close to the Relative Strength Index indicator, most of them are very sensitive to price date and produce a lot of false signals as a result. Option spreads and hybrid strategies benefit from mild path movements.

No Directional Movement

Options traders and investors, especially premium sellers, often seek little to no directional movement. This is due to their desire to profit from premium decay. Similarly, when option traders sell premium, they want a higher volatility level, which lets them get a higher premium for their options sale. This is due to a sharp increase in implied volatility, which expands as volatility rises.

Use Bollinger Bands for Options Trading

The Bollinger Band indicator is another tool for technical analysis in options trading that traders use to define a range-bound market. When the Bollinger Band envelope widens, it indicates a rise in volatility; when the Bollinger Band envelope narrows, it indicates a decline in volatility, and the market is on the verge of being range-bound. When these bands broaden, most options traders sell them, and when they narrow, they buy them.

Another strategy is for traders to use the Bollinger Band as support and resistance when selling premiums beyond the lower and upper bands of the envelope, as these ranges have relatively conservative trading levels on both the downside and upside.

Proven and Practical strategies / from beginner to advanced

Traders often rush into trade options with no knowledge of the options strategies they have. There are several choices that minimize risk and optimize returns. Traders will with a little effort learn how to use the versatility and power supplied by stock options. Here are 10 options that should be known to all investors.

1. Covered Call

One technique for calls is simply to purchase a naked call alternative. A simple protected call or buy-write may also be structured. This is a very common technique because it increases sales and decreases the likelihood that the stock alone will last long. The deal is that you must be prepared to sell your stock at a fixed price – the short strike price. In order to implement the strategy, you buy the underlying stock, and simultaneously write – or sell – a call option on the same shares.

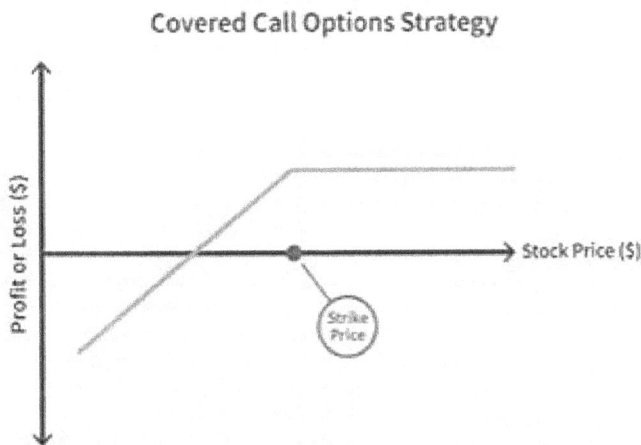

Covered Call Options Strategy

Profit or Loss ($)

Stock Price ($)

Strike Price

For instance, suppose an investor uses an invitational option on a stock that is 100 shares per call option. They will simultaneously offer one call option for every 100 shares of the stock the investor buys. This strategy is known as a covered call because, if an equity price rises quickly, the short call from this investor is covered by the long stock position. Investors may use this technique if they have a short-term stance on the stock and a neutral view of its direction. You may want to create income by selling the call premium or hedge against a possible reduction in the value of the underlying stock.

In the profit and loss graph (P&L) above, the negative P&L from the call is offset by the long share position as the share price rises. The premium received by the investor from selling the call helps the investor to a successful sale of the stock to a higher level than the strike price: the strike price plus the premium received. The P&L graph of the covered call looks a lot like a small, naked P&L graph.

2. Married Put

In a married strategy, an investor buys an asset, like stock shares, and at the same time buys options for equal shares. The option holder shall be entitled to sell stock at the strike price and every offer shall be worth 100 shares.
An investor may opt to use this strategy to protect the danger of a stock's downside. This strategy operates like an insurance policy; when the stock price falls sharply, it sets the price floor.

For example, assume that an investor buys 100 shares and simultaneously buys one option. This strategy will appeal to this investor because it is secured against the downside should a negative price change occur. At the same time, if the stock gains in value, the investor will be able to engage in any incentive. The only downside to this approach is that if the stock does not decrease in value, the investor loses the premium price paid for the bid.

Married Put Options Strategy

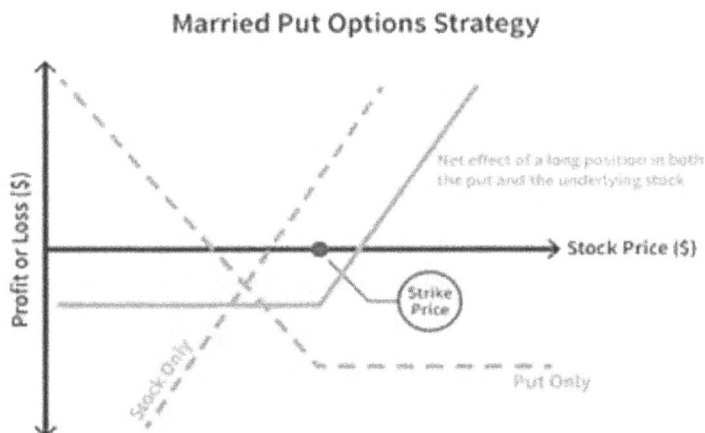

The dotted line is the long stock location in the P&L graph above. Combined with long and long stock positions, the losses are reduced as the stock price declines. However, the stock will take part at the top of the premium paid on the stock. A married P&L graph looks like a long P&L graph.

3. Bull Call Spread

The investor simultaneously buys calls at a given strike price in a torch spread strategy when selling the same number of calls at a higher strike price. The same expiration date and underlying asset will be available for both call options. This form of vertical distribution strategy is used mostly when an investor is bullish with the underlying asset and expects a modest increase in the asset price. This strategy allows investors to restrict their advantages on trade and reduce the net premium they have invested (compared to buying a naked call option outright).

Bull Call Spread Options Strategy

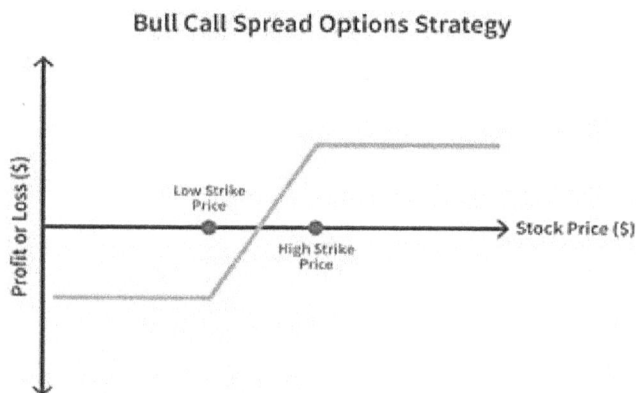

You will notice from the P&L diagram above that this is a bullish approach. To implement this strategy appropriately, the trader requires the stock to raise prices so that it can benefit from the trade. The benefit of a bull call is that your upside is minimal (even though the amount spent on the premium is reduced).
When direct calls are costly, the higher premium can be compensated by selling higher strike calls. This is how a bull's call is made.

4. Bear Put Spread

Another type of vertical spreading is the bear spread strategy. In this strategy, the investor at the same time buys options and sells the same number of puts at a lower impact price. Both options are acquired and have the same expiration date for the same underlying asset. This strategy is applied when the trader has a biased feeling about the asset and expects the price of the asset to decrease. The strategy provides limited losses and limited profits.

Bear Put Spread Options Strategy

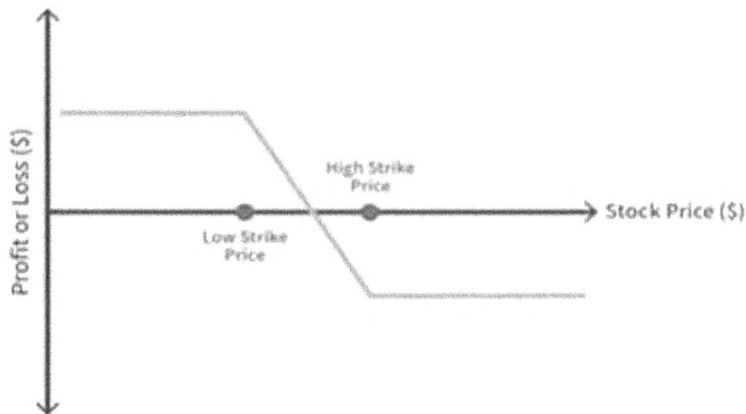

In the above P&L chart, you can see that it is a bizarre technique. In order to enforce this plan effectively, stock prices have to decline. Your upside is minimal when using a bear, but your premium is reduced. If straightforward puts are costly, one way to compensate for high premiums is to offer lower strikes. This is how a bear spread is designed.

5. Protective Collar

A defensive collar policy is carried out with the purchase of an out-of-the-money option and a call-out option. The asset below and the expiry date must be the same. This strategy is frequently used by investors following considerable gains in a long position in a stock. This enables investors to have insurance against the downside, as it helps long-term lock the future selling price. The concession is, however, that they can be forced to sell shares at a higher price and thereby forgo the potential for additional gain.

An example is if an investor has 100 IBM shares for $50 and assumes that IBM will rise to $100 on January 1. The investor could build a protective collar by selling an IBM call on 105 March and at the same time buying one IBM collar on 95 March. The trader is under $95 security before the expiry date. The compromise is that, if IBM trades at that pace before expiry, they will theoretically be obliged to sell their stock at $105.

Protective Collar Options Strategy

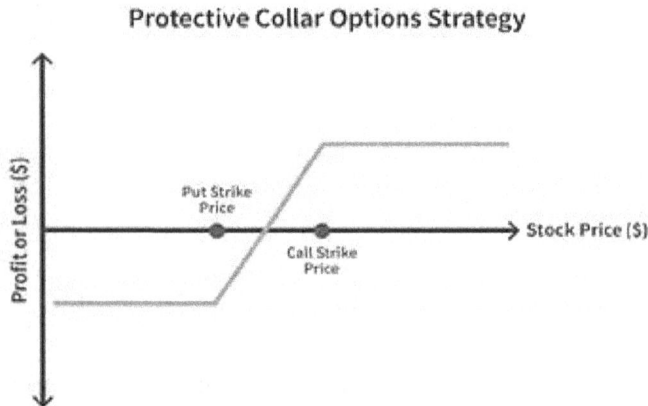

In the P&L diagram above, you will observe that the security collar is a long and covered call combination. This is a neutral trading agreement that will cover the investor in the event of a stock downturn. The offer may have to sell the long stock at the short call hit. The investor would probably be able to do so, however, because they already have returned in the underlying shares.

6. Long Straddle

A strategy for long-range options happens when an investor simultaneously buys a call and options on the same base asset at the same strike price and expiration date. An investor also uses this technique when he thinks that the price of the underlying asset will rise dramatically out of a certain range, but he does not know the direction of the move. In principle, this approach enables the investor to make infinite money. At the same time, its gross losses are limited to the total costs of both options.

Straddle Options Strategy

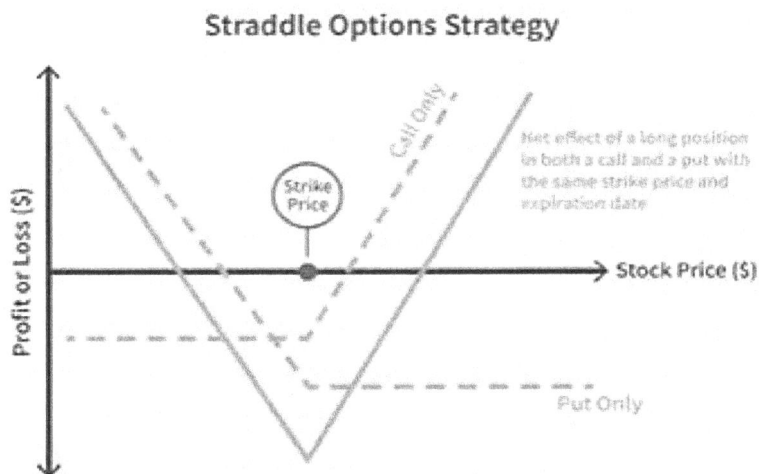

Notice how two breakthrough points exist in the above P&L graph. This strategy is profitable when the stock moves in any direction. The investor is not interested in which direction the stock is moving, but is much more important than the overall premium charged by the investor for the structure.

7. Long Strangle

The investor purchases an out-of-the-money call option in a long-range options strategy, and a money-out option at the same time places the same underlying asset on the same expiration date. An investor who uses the strategy expects that the price of the underlying asset will move in a significant way, but does not know what path the move is going to go.

For example, this strategy may be a wager on earnings news for a corporation or an event relating to the approval of a Pharmaceutical Stock by the Food and Drug Authority (FDA). Losses are limited to the cost of all choices, which are the premium spent. Strangles are almost always cheaper than straddles because the options bought are non-dollar options.

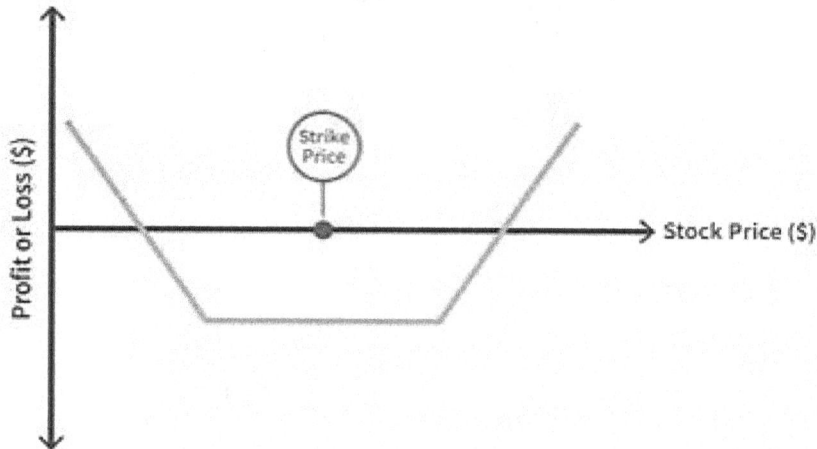

Long Strangle Options Strategy

In the P&L chart above, notice how two breakthrough points exist. This strategy is profitable whether the stock moves in one direction or the other. Again, the investor does not know which way the stock goes, it is just a bigger step than the overall premium charged for the structure by the investor.

8. Long Call Butterfly Spread

Previous tactics allowed two separate roles or contracts to be combined. An investor can mix both a bull spread strategy and a bear spread strategy with a long butterfly spread using call options. Three separate strike prices will also be used. Both options are the same asset and expiry date underlying.

Butterfly Spread Options Strategy

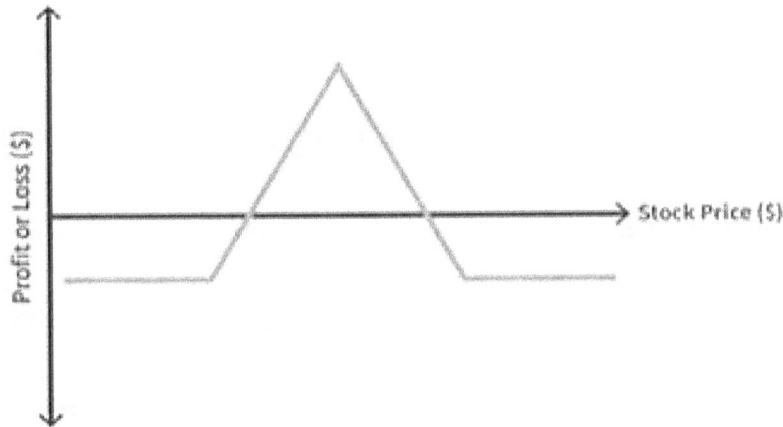

For example, by buying an in-the-money call option at a lower strike price you can make a long butterfly spread while selling two on-the-money call options and buying one on-the-money call option. A balanced butterfly spread has the same width as the wing. This example is called a "call fly" which leads to a net debit. An investor will spread a long butterfly call if he believes that the stock would not move long before expiry.

The P&L chart above shows how the maximum profit is made when the inventory remains unchanged before its expiry–at the time of the ATM attack. As the stock shifts away from the ATM attacks, the more the P&L shift is negative. The maximum loss occurs when the stock is on or below the lower strike (or if the stock settles at or above the higher strike call). The upside and downside of this strategy are minimal.

9. Iron Condor

The investor concurrently owns a bull spread and a bear call in the iron condor strategy. The iron condor is created by selling one out of the money and buying one out of the money in a lower strike – a bull is spread, selling the money and buying a higher call out of the money – a call out. All options have the same expiry date and are on the same asset. The put and call sides usually have the same width. This trading strategy earns a net premium for the structure and is structured to benefit from stock with low volatility. Many traders use this technique because of their perceived high likelihood of a small premium.

Iron Condor Options Strategy

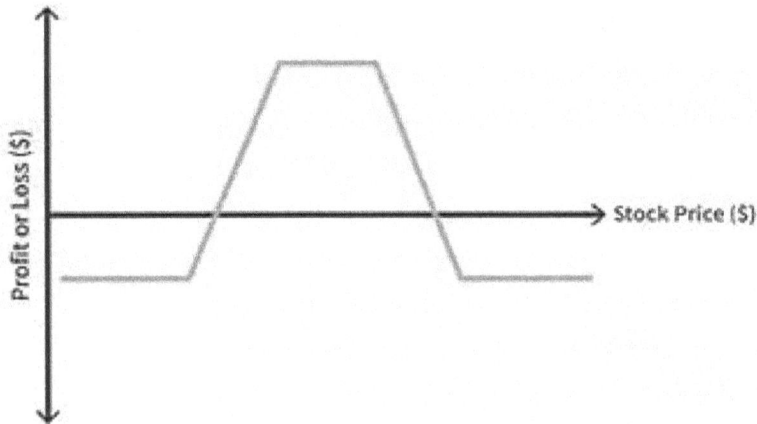

In the above graph P&L, notice how the maximum profit is obtained by keeping the stock in a relatively broad range. The investor will gain the total net credit earned during the construction of the exchange. The more the stock passes through the short strikes – lower for the call and higher – the greater the loss before the highest loss. Usually, the cumulative loss is considerably greater than the maximum gain. This is intuitively rational because the layout is more likely to be finished with a small benefit.

10. Iron Butterfly

In the iron butterfly technique, an investor sells the capital and buys the money. They will also offer an on-the-money call and purchase a cash call at the same time. All options have the same expiry date and are on the same asset. While it is similar to butterfly propagation, it uses calling and calling (as opposed to one or the other).
Essentially, this approach incorporates the sale of a straddle and the purchase of defensive "wings." You can also see the building as two spreads. It is normal for both spreads to have the same width. The long, unpaid call protects from limitless downside. The long, off-the-money defense from the downside (from the short put strike to zero). In accordance with the strike price of the options used, all profit and loss are restricted to a specific range.

Investors like this revenue approach and the increased likelihood of small profits with a

Iron Butterfly Options Strategy

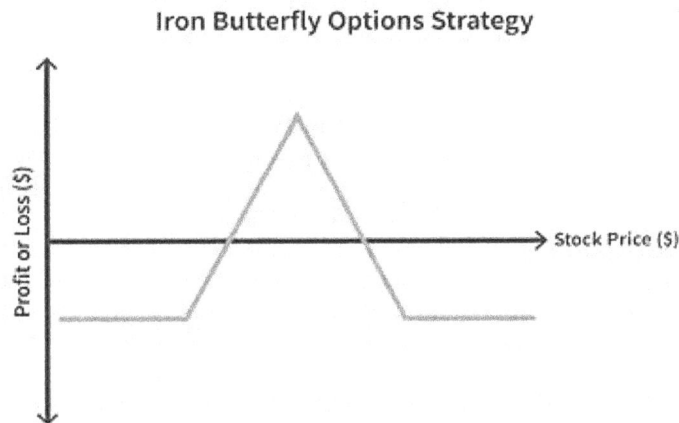

non-volatile stock.

In the P&L chart above, note that the maximum benefit is produced when the stock remains in the financial strikes of both the call and the call. The overall benefit is the gross net premium. Maximum loss occurs if the stock moves above or below the long call strike.

How to Maximize Returns / Minimize Risks

Many investors erroneously conclude that options are always riskier than stocks because they do not understand precisely what options are and how they operate. Options may actually be used to hedge positions and reduce risks, such as a safeguard. Options may also be used to bet on a stock that rises or falls but is comparatively less risky than owning or shortening the actual stock equivalent. The emphasis of this article is on this latter use of options to mitigate risk in making directional bets. Read on to quantify the possible risk of options and how the leverage capacity will work for you.

Options and Leverage

Let us first understand the leverage principle and how it relates to options. Leverage has two fundamental concepts for the trading of options. The first is to use the same sum of money to take a larger spot. This is the term that causes investors the most difficulty. A stock dollar and the same dollar an option invested are not the same risks.
The second concept defines leverage as retaining the same scale but spending less money. This is the concept of leverage incorporated into its frame of reference by a consistently active trader or investor.

Interpretation of the numbers

Consider the example below. You intend to spend $10 thousand in a 50 dollars stock but are tempted to purchase $10 alternative contracts. After all, an investment of $10,000 in $10 allows you to purchase 10 contracts (100 shares) and to control 1,000 shares. In the meantime, only 200 shares will be bought in the $50 stock for $10,000.

In this case, trade-in options are riskier than the trade-in stocks. Your whole investment with the stock trade will only be lost if the price is unlikely to shift from $50 to $0. However, if the stock drops to the strike price, you will lose your entire investment in the options market. So, if the Options Strike price is $40 (an option for the money), the stock must only fall below $40 by the expiry of the investment, although it is only a 20% decrease.

There is a significant risk difference between stocks and options of the same dollar sum. This risk imbalance occurs because the correct leverage term has been incorrectly applied. Let us explore two ways to balance risk disparity while holding positions fairly profitable to correct this confusion.

Calculation of conventional risk

The first technique for balancing risk disparities is the most common and traditional approach. Let us return to our example to see how it works:

You will earn 200 shares if you invested $10,000 in a stock of $50. Instead of buying 200 shares, two call option contracts may be purchased. You pay less money by buying the options, but still, manage the same amount of shares. In other words, the number of options is determined by the number of shares that the investment capital may have purchased.

Tell us your plan to purchase 1,000 XYZ shares at $41,75 for a cost of $41,750. However, you can buy 10 call option contracts, with a strike price of $30 (in the money) per contract, instead of buying the stock at $41,75. The buying options would include a gross capital expenditure of $16,300 for 10 calls. This means a net savings of $25,450 or nearly 60 percent of your shares.

This saving of $25,450 can be used in a variety of ways. First, you should take advantage of other opportunities and diversify further. Secondly, it can only sit on a trading account and collect cash market prices. Interest collection will generate the so-called synthetic dividend. For example, if the $25,450 savings receive 2% interest on a money market account every year. During the lifetime of the option, the account earns $509 interest per year or about $42 per month.

Now you are, in a way, collecting a dividend on a stock that cannot pay one as you take advantage of the options. Best of all, this can be done with about one-third of the money required to buy the stock in full.

Calculation of alternative risk

The other solution to balance costs and disparities in size is risk-based.
As we have found, buying $10,000 in stock is not the same as buying $10,000 in risk options. Exposure to options is much more dangerous as loss probability is significantly increased. You must have a risk-equivalent position in relation to the inventory position to match the playing field.
Let us start by purchasing 1,000 shares for a total investment of $41,750, which is $41,750. As a risk-conscious investor, you also enter a stop-loss order, a conservative technique recommended by experts in the industry.
You set an order at a price that reduces your loss to 20 percent of your investment to $8,350. If this is the amount you are prepared to sacrifice, it should be the amount you are prepared to spend on an option role as well. In other words, you can pay just $8,350 to purchase risk equivalence options. In this technique, you are at risk for the same dollar sum as you were willing to lose in-stock position.
If you have stock, stop orders won't protect you from opening up gaps. Once the stock opens below the strike price, you lost everything you can lose - that is, the total amount you spent buying your calls. If you own the stock, you will lose even more, but the position of the options is less risky than the position of the stock.
Tell yourself you are buying $60 of a biotech stock, and it falls below $20 if the company's drug kills a test patient. Your stop order will be executed at $20, which will result in a disastrous loss of $40. In this situation, your stop order did not afford much security. However, claim that you transfer stock ownership and purchase the $11.50 call options instead. Your risk scenario is now changing drastically because you risk just the amount of money you paid for this choice. Therefore, when the stock opens at $20, your mates who purchased the stock get $40, and you lose $11.50. When used in this way, options become less risky than stocks.

Ways to Minimize Risk And Maximize Profit In Options

There are many ways you can increase profits and mitigate risks. Some of them are here:
- Use limit orders and stop-limit orders. You may position a limit order to enter a trade in the price you want, or a stop order or stop order to limit your losses or to lock your benefit. Remember this rule: stop losing trades fast and allow winning trades to run as far as you can.

- Diversify your portfolio, if it is good to invest only in one stock, but increase the risk. Try to invest in various industries and tools (bonds, real estate, commodities, ETFs, etc.).

- Follow the industry trend. By merely trading in the same direction, we are already on the side of higher likelihood.

- Trade always in accordance with your plan, strategy.

- You don't need consistency, not quantity, over the exchange. You also spend more money on fees when you deal with business.

- Using the risk to pay in every trade to decide whether a trade is worth taking and to know when you can leave if the business is unsuccessful.

- Follow your money management plan, never allow yourself in any single period to lose more than a certain amount of money.

- Don't depend on only one predictor. Use as much as possible and then decide the final answer. This will provide you with a better understanding of what could happen.

- When you invest on a long-term basis, research the company you buy or sell before you open and close the spot. If you do this, you're more likely to be right.

- Create a business plan to help you set your goals and keep them focused.

- Know the market enough that you can foresee what happens with future rates. For example: if in New York, you want to rent houses and assess the piece of land that you purchase, you can ask questions such as whether the location is good? Has it a good neighborhood?

- Last but not least, be prepared and learn all the information you can.

Different Type of Charts Used in Technical Analysis

Technical analysis is incomplete without maps. They are the backbone upon which every analytical effort is built. In this article, we'll look at the four (+1) main forms of technical research charts that are most widely used to extract useful knowledge about a specific asset. The following are the details:

Line Charts: The line chart is the most basic type of chart in technical analysis, and it is created by joining the closing prices of an asset over a given time span. Many investors consider the closing price to be the most relevant data point, so this type of charting technique gives it more weight. This often assists the analyst in filtering out the "noise" and creating a more coherent picture. On the other hand, the chartist misses out on the complexities of price fluctuations on lower time frames, which could have been studied more extensively using a different charting style.
A line chart of Tata Power is shown below.

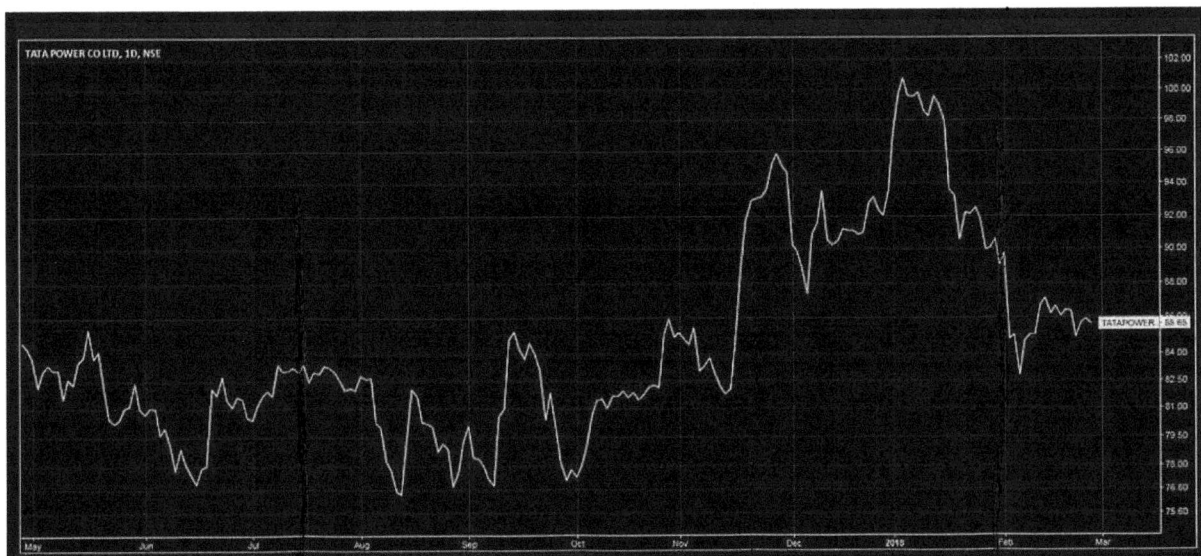

TATA POWER CO LTD, 1D, NSE

Bar Chart: The bar chart, which considers a security's open, high, and low prices as well as its closing price, is an improvement over the simple line chart. In technical analysis, this type of chart shows us where the stock opened and closed, as well as the high and low points for that trading time, and therefore the day's range. Also, by examining the day's closing price, one can determine if the protection is controlled by buyers or sellers. A horizontal dash on the left side shows the day's opening price. A horizontal dash on the right side also signifies the end of the session. A vertical line connects the day's high and low points.

The bar is colored green if the close is greater than the open. If the close is less than the open, the bar will be colored red.

A bar chart of the same Tata Power line chart as in the previous example is shown below.

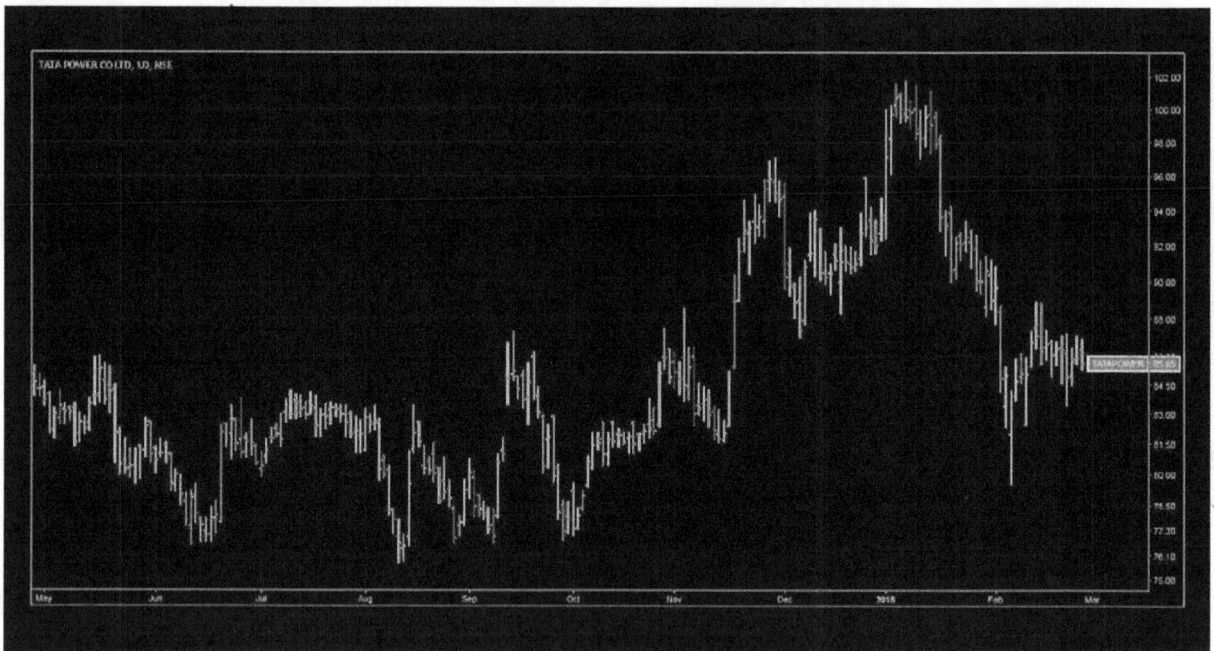

TATA POWER CO LTD, 1D, NSE

Candlestick Charts: Candlestick charts are the most commonly used charting technique by technical traders all over the world. Established by a Japanese rice trader named Munehisa Homma in the 18th century, this charting technique has its roots in the 18th century. Steve Nison later brought candlestick charting to western countries through his book Japanese Candlestick Charting Techniques.

The visual component of perception is the most visible difference between a bar chart and a candlestick chart. Candlestick charts are much more physically appealing than bar charts, and they often communicate the fundamental psychology of market investors on a specific financial instrument.

Many candlestick designs, such as a Dragonfly Doji, a Hammer, or a Dark Cloud Cover, have been given catchy names that all convey a strong meaning to the chartist.

The only distinction between this and bar charts is the 'real body' of a candle, which is represented by a vertical rectangle formed by joining the opening and closing prices. We get a hollow/white/green candle if the closing price is higher than the opening price. A filled/black/red candle is formed when the closing price is less than the opening price.

A candlestick chart of Tata Power is shown below. This is the same map like the one above, but with a different charting style.

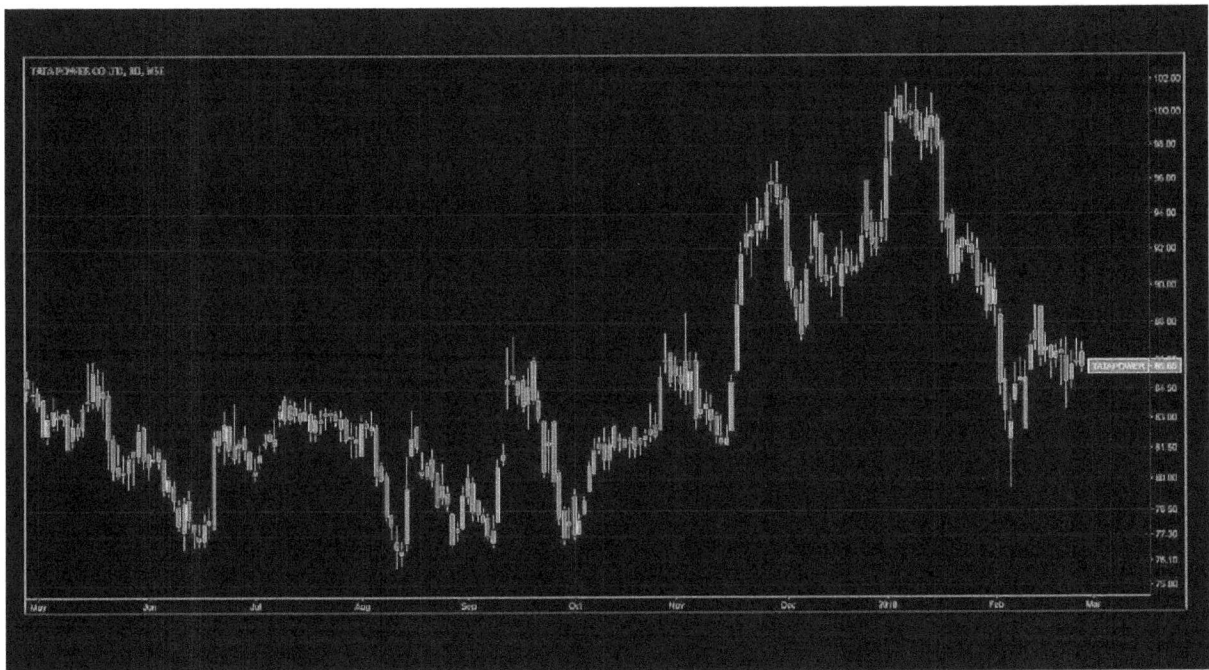

Point and Figure Charts: For the average investor, these charts are always a foreign language. They are, however, very good at filtering out chart noise. These types of maps, which place a greater focus on price, ignore the time and volume factors.

A set of Xs and Os make up a point and figure map. The Xs represent increasing prices, while the Os represent decreasing prices. A new X or an O is added to the sequence only when a stock moves by a certain number of points. This is known as the 'box size,' and it varies from one stock to the next, with the trader or analyst settling on it arbitrarily to suit his or her needs.

A point and figure chart of the same financial instrument that we saw earlier is shown below. Owing to the use of this cutting-edge charting method, it appears to be very different here.

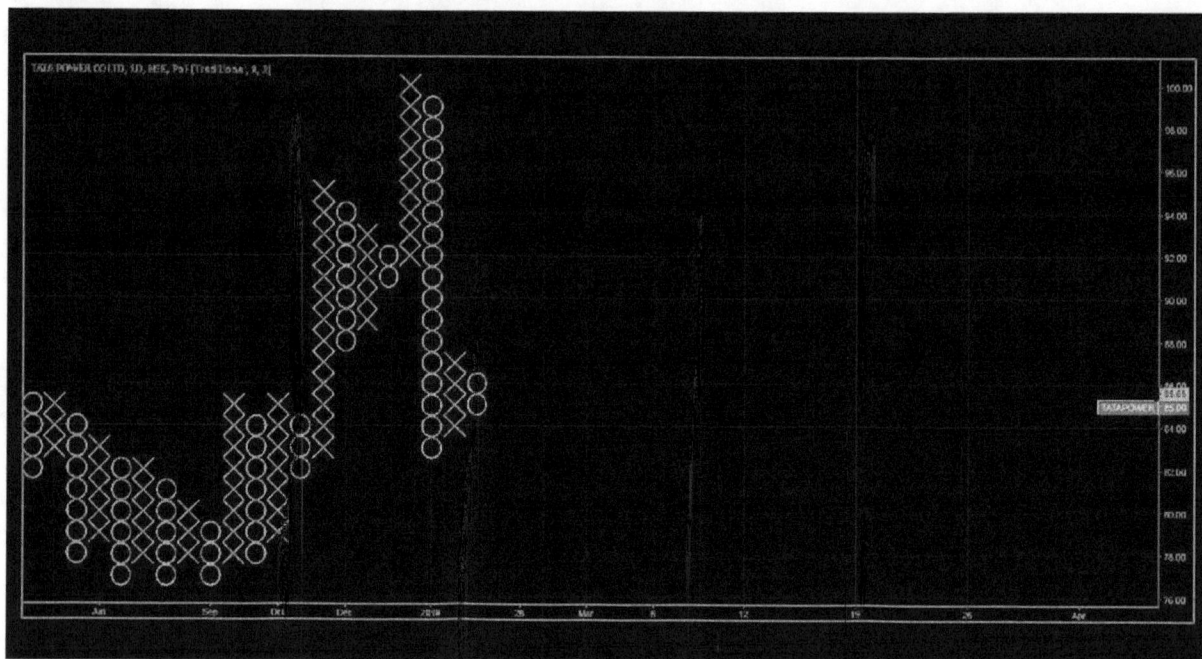

OHLC Chart

An OHLC chart is a form of bar chart that displays each period's open, high, low, and closing prices. OHLC charts are useful because they show the four main data points over time, with many traders finding the closing price to be the most relevant.

Since it can display rising or declining momentum, this chart form is useful. Where the open and close are far apart, it indicates strong momentum, while when they are close together, it indicates indecision or poor momentum. The high and low points reflect the entire price range of the time, which is useful for calculating volatility. On OHLC charts, traders search for many trends.

OHLC Charts: What You Need to Know

A vertical line and two short horizontal lines running to the left and right of the horizontal line make up an OHLC map. The opening price for the period is defined by the horizontal line extending to the left, while the closing price for the period is represented by the horizontal line extending to the right. The period's intraday range is reflected by the vertical line's height, with the high representing the period's high and the low representing the period's low. A price bar is a name given to the entire structure. Since the close is above the open, the right line would be above the left as the price increases over time. These bars are frequently black in color. Since the close is below the open, the right line would be below the left if the price falls during the time. These bars are usually red in color.

Any time frame can be used for OHLC maps. When added to a 5-minute map, the open, high, low, and close prices for each 5-minute duration will be shown. It will display the open, big, low, and close price for each day if added to a regular map.

Line charts only display closing prices linked into a continuous line, while OHLC charts show more detail. OHLC and candlestick charts both show the same amount of data, but in slightly different ways. Although OHLC charts use left and right-facing horizontal lines to display the open and close, candlestick charts use a real body to show the open and close.

How to Read OHLC Charts

When it comes to interpreting OHLC maps, professional analysts use a variety of methods. Here are a few pointers.

Vertical Height: The vertical height of an OHLC bar represents the period's uncertainty. If the line-height is very high, traders know that the market is very volatile and indecisive.

Horizontal Line Location: Technical traders can say where the asset opened and closed relative to its high and low by looking at the position of the left and right horizontal lines. Traders may conclude that the rally fizzled near the end of the time if the security rallied higher but the close was far lower than the maximum. Selling fizzled out towards the end of the time if the price dropped but closed much higher than its low.

When the open and close are close together, it suggests indecision because the price could not rise much in either direction. If the close is significantly higher or lower than the open, it indicates that there was significant selling or buying during the time.

During an uptrend, there would usually be more black bars than red bars. During a downtrend, there are typically more red bars than black bars. This will reveal details about the trend's intensity and course. At first glance, a series of broad black bars suggests strong upward movement. Although further research is needed, this knowledge may be useful in determining whether or not to dig deeper into the data.

Patterns: Traders keep an eye out for patterns on the OHLC chart. The central reversal, inside bar, and outside bar are the three main patterns. When the price opens above the prior bar's close, makes a new high, and then closes below the prior bar's low, it is considered a key reversal in an uptrend. It indicates a significant change in momentum, which may signal the start of a pullback. When the price opens below the previous bar's close, makes a new low, and then closes above the prior bar's high, it is considered a key reversal in a downtrend. This suggests a strong upward change, signaling the likelihood of a rally.

An OHLC chart example

The OHLC chart for the S&P 500 SPDR ETF is shown below (SPY). Overall increases, such as the one seen at the beginning of October, are normally followed by a larger number of black bars. The price moves marginally higher but mostly sideways through mid-November, with more alternating bar colors.

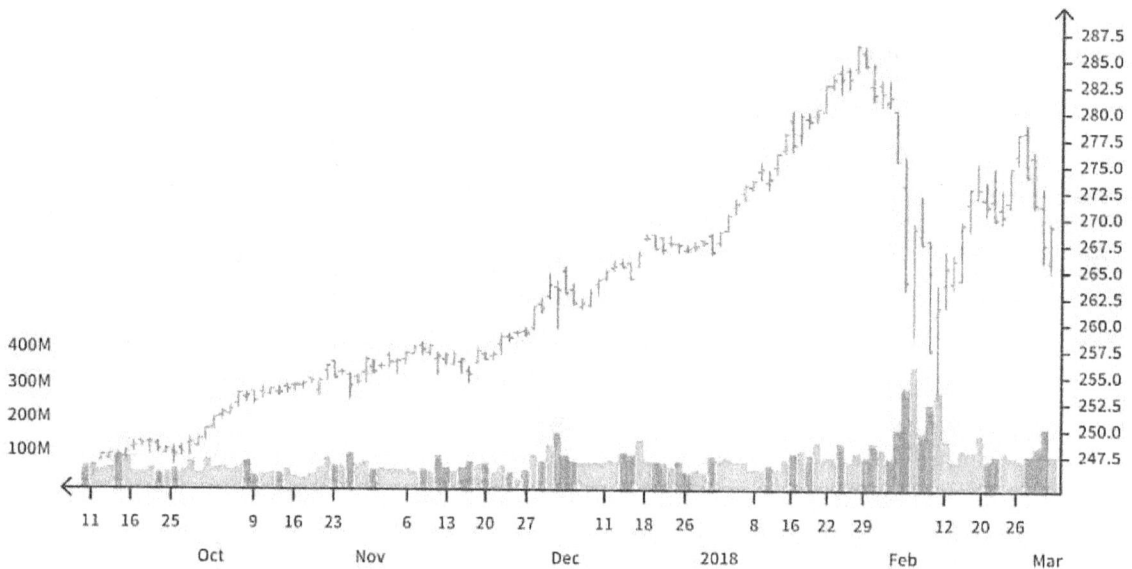

The price begins to increase in mid-November, as demonstrated by a couple of wider-ranging black bars. The price started to rise at the start of the year, dominated by black rising bars. There are big red bars at the start of February, much larger than those seen during the previous advance. This is a huge indicator of intense selling pressure.

How to Choose A Broker

Here's a step-by-step guide to finding a broker that can meet your options trading needs in terms of service and account features.

1. Seek out a free educational opportunity.

Finding a broker with educational tools is important if you're new to options trading or want to extend your trading strategies. This education can take many forms, such as:

- Online options trading courses.

- Live or recorded webinars.

- One-on-one guidance online or by phone.

- Face-to-face meetings with a larger broker that has branches across the country.

It's a good idea to go into student mode for a while and pick up as much information and advice as possible. Even better, if a broker provides a simulated version of its options trading platform, use a paper trading account to run through the process before losing any real money.

2. Put the customer service of your broker to the test.

Especially for newer options traders, dependable customer service should be a top priority. It's also crucial for those swapping brokers or performing complicated trades that need assistance.

Consider your preferred method of touch. Is it possible to have a live online chat? If you have an email address? Is it possible to get assistance by phone? Is there a dedicated trading desk available at the broker? What are the staffing hours? Is technical support available 24 hours a day, seven days a week, or only on weekdays? What about members who can answer your account-related questions?

Reach out and ask any questions before applying for an account to see if the responses and response time are sufficient.

3. Ensure that the trading platform is simple to use.

Platforms for trading options come in a variety of sizes and shapes. They can be web- or software-based, have different channels for simple and advanced trading, provide complete or partial mobile features, or a combination of the above.

Look for a guided tour of a broker's network and software on its website. Screenshots and video guides are helpful, but checking out a broker's virtual trading platform, if one exists, can give you the best idea of whether or not the broker is a good match.

Find the following:

- Is the platform architecture intuitive, or do you have to search and peck to find what you're searching for?

- Is it simple to make a trade?

- Is the platform capable of performing tasks such as generating warnings based on particular requirements or enabling you to fill out a trade ticket ahead of time and apply it later?

- Will you need complete access to the platform while you're on the go, or will a trimmed-down version suffice?

- How trustworthy is the platform, and how quickly are orders fulfilled?

If your approach includes rapidly entering and leaving positions, this is a top priority. Is there a monthly or annual platform fee charged by the broker? If that's the case, are there any ways to avoid paying the charge, such as maintaining a minimum account balance or making a certain number of trades in a given time frame?

4. Analyze the data and resources in terms of their scope, depth, and expense.

The lifeblood of an options trader is data and analysis. The following are some of the most important things to search for:

- A quote feed that is updated on a regular basis.

- Basic charting to assist you in determining your entry and exit points.

- The ability to determine the costs and benefits of a deal (maximum upside and maximum downside).

Screening Tools

Deeper analytical and trade modeling tools, such as customizable screeners, the ability to develop, test, monitor, and back-test trading strategies, and real-time market data from multiple providers, may be required by those pursuing more advanced trading strategies. Check to see if the deluxe pieces are extra. Many brokers, for example, offer free delayed quotes that are 20 minutes behind market data but charge a fee for real-time quotes. Similarly, certain pro-level resources may be restricted to customers who meet certain trading activity or account balance minimums on a monthly or quarterly basis.

5. Don't put too much emphasis on the cost of commissions.

There's a reason why commission fees are at the bottom of our chart. Price isn't anything, and it isn't nearly as significant as the other factors we've discussed. However, since commissions allow for a simple side-by-side comparison, they are often the first considerations when choosing an options broker.

There are a few things to keep in mind when it comes to how much brokers charge to trade options:

The base rate — which is exactly the same as the trading commission that investors pay when they buy a portfolio — and the per-contract charge are the two components of an options-trading commission. Commissions have dropped dramatically in recent years; many brokers now pay no commissions, and contract fees range from $.50 to $1 per contract.

Some brokers charge a single flat fee that includes both the trading commission and the per-contract fee.

Some brokers can give you a discount on commissions or contract fees if you trade regularly, have a high number of trades, or have a high average account balance. The term "high volume" or "active trader" is described differently by each brokerage.

If you're new to options trading or just use it occasionally, you may be better off going with a broker that charges a single flat rate on all trades or one that doesn't charge a commission (you won't be able to stop the per-contract fee). If you're a more aggressive trader, consider whether a tiered pricing package will save you money.

Portfolio Management

Portfolio management is the art and science of choosing and managing a group of investments that meets customer, business, or organization long-term financial goals and risk tolerance.

Portfolio management needs the ability to assess strengths and weaknesses, opportunities, and risks across the entire investment spectrum. The choices include compensation, ranging from debt to equity, to domestic, to foreign, and growth vs security.

Professional licensed portfolio managers work on behalf of investors, while individuals may choose to create and maintain their own portfolios. In any case, the overall objective of the portfolio manager is to optimize the anticipated return on assets at a reasonable degree of risk exposure.

The management of portfolios may be passive or active in nature.

Passive management is a long-term approach that is described and forgotten. It may include investing in one or more ETF index funds. This is generally known as indexing or index spending. Those who create indexed portfolios will use modern portfolio theory (MPT) to optimize the combination.

Active management means trying to overcome the index's performance through the active purchase and distribution of individual inventories and other properties. In general, closed-end funds are actively controlled. Active managers can use a variety of quantitative or qualitative models in their assessment of potential investments.

Important of Portfolio Management

Allocation of assets

The long-term asset mix is the secret to successful portfolio management. In general, this means inventories, bonds, and "money," such as deposit certificates. Others are commonly referred to as alternative investments, such as property, commodities, and derivatives.

The distribution of assets is based on the awareness that different types of assets are not mixed and that some are more volatile than other assets. A mix of assets offers balance and safeguards against risk.

Investors who weigh their portfolios more aggressively on more risky assets, such as growth stocks. Conservative investors weigh their holdings on stable investments such as bonds and blue chips.

Diversification

The only truth in investing is that winners and losers cannot be predicted consistently. The cautious approach is to build an investment basket that offers a large exposure within an asset class.

Diversification spreads risk and reward across a class of assets. Differentiation aims to capture the returns of all sectors over time while reducing uncertainty at all times as it is difficult to know which subset of an asset class or sector is likely to outperform another. Real diversification is achieved by different types of shares, economic sectors, and geographical regions.

Rebalancing

Rebalancing is used to return a portfolio periodically, usually annually, to its initial target allocation. This is done to restore the original asset mix if it is driven out by market fluctuations.

For example, a portfolio that begins with 70 percent equity and 30 percent fixed-income allocation might transition to an 80/20 allocation after an extended market rally. The investor has made a decent profit but now there is more risk in the portfolio than the investor can bear.

In general, rebalancing means selling high-priced securities and bringing this capital into cheaper and out-of-favor securities.

The annual rebalancing exercise helps investors to catch profits and increase the chance for growth in high potential sectors while holding their portfolios in line with the original risk/return profile.

Active Portfolio Management

An active management strategy is used by fund managers or brokers to purchase and sell inventories and try to outperform a particular index, such as the Standard & Poor's 500 Index or the Russell 1000 Index.

An active investment fund has a single portfolio manager, co-managers, or a team of managers who actively decide on the investment fund. The success of an active fund depends on a combination of in-depth analysis, market forecasts, and portfolio managers' or management team's expertise.

Portfolio managers involved in active management concentrate closely on market dynamics, developments in the economy, policy environment changes, and news impacting businesses. This data is used in order to take advantage of inconsistencies when purchasing or selling investments. Active managers say that these processes increase the return potential by merely imitating holdings on a certain index.

Trying to conquer the competition obviously implies additional risk to the market. Indexing removes this specific danger, as there can be no human error in the selection of stocks. Index funds are often traded less often, which means they have lower spending rates and are more tax-efficient than active funds.

Passive Portfolio Management

The aim of passive portfolio management is to duplicate the return of a certain market index or benchmark, often referred to as index fund management. Managers buy the same stocks listed on the index using the same weighting as the index.

A passive portfolio of strategies can be organized as an ETF, a mutual fund, or as a trust in a unit of investment. Index funds are branded as actively managed as they each have a portfolio manager who is responsible for replicating the index and not for purchasing or selling the assets.

Usually, investment charges on passive investments or funds are much smaller than active management strategies.

Most Famous Trading Platforms

Options trading gives online brokers considerably higher profit margins than stock trading, which makes competition fierce to attract these customers. This kind of business environment is excellent for traders because healthy competition fuels product creativity. Each broker is the best platform for trading options.

Here are some checked trading platforms for 2021. Our testing was based on options chains (for example, optional views, total optional columns, data streaming efficiency, total Greek options), analysis of options (for example, P&L charts, calculators), and management of positions of choice (e.g., if greeks stream, rolling functionality, grouping availability, and advanced position analysis). With most brokers offering similar prices, commercial costs have not affected our score.

Best Trading Platforms for Options 2021

The best trading platforms based on more than 30 variables are here.

- E*TRADE
- TradeStation
- TD Ameritrade
- Charles Schwab
- Interactive Brokers
- Tradeking

- Option Station Pro
- Trade Station Mobile
- First Trade

How to Understand When Enter or Exit from The Market

The profitability of an options trade is largely depending on the accuracy of the rates at which it is entered and left. Since $.10-per-cent to $10.00-per-cent changes in the value are so common, the profit or loss made in a stock trade is negligible, but in an option trade it may be worth a big. This means that you pay $2 for the right to sell shares and $3 for the privilege to exercise them. The return of fifty percent reflects $1.50 in profit per share. The $.10 decrease in price had greatly benefited the company and the $.10 increase in exit price had given it a nice gain, resulting in a profit of $.63 per share, representing a significantly improved 63% return.
The argument is that in options trading, getting good prices is very important. The difference between the lower and the buy-in fee or exit fee covers the costs on both sides of the exchange

As in all things, prices are first driven by supply and demand, options are often going up and down.
Usually, stock and ETF prices are quoted in $1-cent increments. The same framework is applied to some but not all choices. Most stocks are priced in dollars, but this isn't always the case. Many trades over $3 will be priced by $.05 or $.10, but for those who cost $3 or more, there will be cases where the pricing is by $.05 or more.10 increments. It is possible for certain large volume stock and ETF options to have as much as $0.01 price increments if the overall price of the stock is $3.00 or higher.01.

When you offer a quote, use both your bid and the ask prices.
Each option will have a market price (the "Bid" price) and a non-market price (the "Ask") set by an exchange. Bid is the highest option price an individual (or market maker) trader (or seller) is willing to accept The Ask is the lowest price at which some traders would buy an option. in most places, you'll just see the best bid and ask rates that were collected from the various exchanges
It is a common misconception that the Ask often exceeds the Bid. The Ask/Bid discrepancy is called the 'spread' and is usually referred to as the difference between two values. Depending on the liquidity of the spread will be between a dollar and two dollars for the options that are less liquid. Whenever the Spread is big, you can be able to get a better deal between the Buy and the Sell prices.

Remember: When the Ask and Bid values are equal, the Spread would be higher than 15 percent. Tradeable volumes should be tracked to ensure adequate liquidity is available.

The spread of an option is regulated by the market, not the option writer He makes his money by using a spread that is adequate. He is aiming to find someone who is eager to purchase an option, and also eager to sell the same option. Two alternatives cancel each other and the market maker pockets an equal amount of money and takes an equal role in the market. Even a small profits accumulate into huge sums of money in the long run.

In a high-volume market where demand for both option purchases and sales is low, the market maker is satisfied with a narrow Spread because it's simple to balance his long and short positions and get the money without incurring price volatility. At a very high demand for an alternative, or in a low supply, the market maker holds a large Spread. It is difficult to find a counterparty in the Matching Market when risk is high.
Let's now look at how to get into and out of a trade. to simply a long place we'll confine ourselves to opening and closing options Thus, we mean that it is finished "first in, first out" or "first in, first out."

Entering a Trade

There are two primary ways to reach an option order: purchasing or selling options on their opening. Usually, an option is purchased through a market order or a limit order. For most options traders, the rule is to not place a market order in the opening period of the day. The most you can hope for is to be supplied at the bid price you are willing to pay, but sometimes you will be dissatisfied. if you are placing an order for many contracts, several will be filled by the low offer, while the others will rise until the remaining offers are exhausted.
In a volatile economy, you can only survive by using a market order. Under such circumstances, you are putting yourself in the position of being at the mercy of the market manipulator, who has tremendous latitude when market orders are filled.

Limit orders are still by far the most common way to buy options. There is a limit order in which you can specify an option that allows you to choose the cheapest price. When you place the limit order, you choose the amount you're willing to pay for the option and enter the price you want. Your order will or price will be rejected, but only if you don't have enough money to pay for it. To determine an appropriate price to position a limit order, we will review some recent trades.

The opening price is $2.42, which translates to a Bid-Ask price of $2.42 and an Ask price of $2. There's no give in this. Spread price: $2.97 There is a rule that spreads are closed only for deep-in-in-the-the-the-money options. When you place a stop-loss order to sell at $2.42, you will usually receive a fast fill.

For example, the market price of Bid is $2.40 and the asking price is $2.60. With a Spread of $20, we have some leeway. Or you might try to divide the balance at $2.50 per share, limiting the purchase of this position to two-thirds of the shares available. It can be a struggle to get 'stuffed' at that price. Moving the price above $2.55 increases your chances of being filled.

For example, **#3A**, the bid is $4.00 and the ask is $4.40 The floor option is trading at $3 a minimum of $.05, making it more likely that the spread will be no less than $.05. Suggests a wiggle room of $30 is possible in this bet. The typical aim of a "limit order to buy" is to sacrifice the rest of the spread. An option that would be more practical would be to put a conservative cap order at $4.30. This has a $.20:0.20 profit for the market maker, which would be sufficient to obtain a trade.

This example gives the Bid price of $8.50 and the Ask price of $9.10. With a deeper-in-in-the-the-the-money option, you could get the same deal. Although the market maker is not really interested in trading this option, it will still be profitable for him to do so, since it is exceptionally large. To increase your odds of getting a higher selling price, don't hesitate to put on a fight for the sale.

Exiting a Trade

The practice of closing an option position is known as a 'closing the option.' It can be achieved in one of two ways: either by a business order or a limit order in the market. It is also worthwhile to explore two alternative methods of exiting an options trade: either with a stop-loss order or a limit order.

The majority of options traders employ an urgent escape strategy when it seems absolutely necessary to protect themselves from significant loss. The sale price you earn when you place a market order to sell an option will likely be less than the offer.

When trading with a limit order, the order can be compared to a new position as you have entered the market. You settle on a price that you think is fair to ask and join it. If you do, you're getting your fill, it must be better than that. Let's use numbers 1-3A to explain the protocol for when to put a limit order on an exit.

The first trading example: The asking price is $2.42 and the bid price is $2.42. There is no wiggle room. Spread price: $2.97 Once you place a sale order for $2.40, you will most likely get a fast response.

This is a good example of an auction bid of $2.40 and an ask of $2.60, which is on sale for $2. With a Spread of $20, we have some leeway. Alternatively, you might place a split order to set a price at $2.50. It can be a struggle to get 'stuffed' at that price. The more you lower the price, the more customers are likely to buy.

Example #3B: It's demanding $4.40, with a bid of $4.10. The floor option is trading at $3 a minimum of $.05, making it more likely that the spread will be no less than $.05. Suggests a wiggle room of $30 is possible in this bet. In general, a maximum order to the sale must be more than a limit. The most to put a limit order at $4.20 at a premium This has a $.20:0.20 profit for the market maker, which would be sufficient to obtain trade.

Let's then review a stop-loss order for the purchase of an option. To trigger an order, specify a trigger price to which will fire it. When either I the option trades at the strike price or below, or (ii) when you inquire. The choice is now executed. If this is an unfilled order, the fill will be of exactly the same price as the bid. Avoid the use of this form unless the possibility of significant loss.

At the end of the day, the one which has the limit order to sell an option should be checked. Like a stop order, you indicate a trigger price. In addition, you set a maximum selling price for your long options here. It is defined in exactly the same way as for the stop-loss order. One order must be activated for the price to be different from the other. Running a stop order can be complicated Both your trigger price ceiling and your floor must be carefully measured in order to give yourself the best chance of a sale. You'll have a shortage if you set the limit price too close to the previous sales price, or lower that you might not get a particularly good deal when you really want to satisfy the customer's need. Let's take a hypothetical situation:

Example #1C: You are already paying $4.00 for a long-minute phone call Keep an upper limit on this place to a stop price to avoid selling this option for $3.50 or less Set a trigger price of $3.60, and set a limit of $3.50 as a theoretical maximum. It could occur that the option price is such that the buyer is now willing to pay $3.60 for the right to buy and the seller $3.40 for the obligation to sell. Your asking price ($3.50) has been set, so your limit order to sell is now active. Since the Bid is lower than your quota, unfortunately, you will not be able to fill your order.

It's a good idea to equalize the trigger price and the limit price to account for expected order fill prices. The trigger was set to $3.70 in order to compensate for a 20% dollar spread in the seller's favor, or $3.70 to account for a 20 dollar spread in the price difference between the two values. When the asking price reaches $3.50 and the bid price reaches $3.70, your order to sell will be made executable at that price." At your target price of $3.50, this is much better.

How To Exit An Options Trade

When it comes to exiting an options trade (that is, buying to close or selling to close), there are a few options. We'll go through the various ways you can take care of the closing end of your trade-in this segment.

Stop-Loss Order

The stop-loss order specifies a price level at which you'd like to leave the exchange, which is typically used to reduce losses. When trading options, you can set your stop-loss depending on the stock's price or the option's price. Your stop-loss will convert to a market order after this "trigger" price is reached, and the trade will be conducted at the current available market price. If the stock or option price moves rapidly, your real exit price can vary dramatically from your stop-loss trigger. As a result, although the stop-loss ensures a reasonably quick exit from the exchange, it does not ensure a specific exit price.

Stop-Limit Order

When activated, the stop-limit order translates to a limit order rather than a market order, giving you more leverage over your exit. To put it another way, the stop-limit defines a minimum or maximum price at which the order can be enforced, ensuring that you are not penalized by a constantly shifting option premium. However, as in any other limit order, if the requisite conditions aren't met, the order cannot be enforced.

One-Cancels-Other

The one-cancels-other (OCO) order, which is actually two orders, allows you to prepare for two separate situations. The other order is immediately canceled when one of the parameters is reached and the corresponding order is executed.

You should prepare to exit a role after it has surpassed either your target benefit or your maximum reasonable loss in this way. When one of these thresholds is reached, half of the OCO is carried out according to your instructions. The other half of the OCO is immediately canceled until the process is completed.

Deadly Mistakes and Pitfalls to Avoid

Once you understand the fundamental principles, trading options isn't difficult. When used correctly, they can be extremely useful, but when used incorrectly, they can be extremely harmful.

You could benefit if stocks go up, down, or sideways, and these wonderful opportunities could lead you to make costly mistakes in options trading. Despite how tempting this sounds, you might lose all of your money if you participate in options trading. And you can do this in a short period of time.

Is that anything you want? Obviously not. No one wants to be in a position where they are unable to make a profit. So, what are our options?

It's critical to comprehend how and why options traders make mistakes, as well as how to stop them. Even the most seasoned traders can make mistakes when it comes to options trading. They can misunderstand an opportunity, be less cautious, and make mistakes in options trading due to almost any lack of attention.

We'll look at the most common blunders, how to stop them, and how to solve them. Beginner options traders are prone to making these errors. So, take the time to assess them so you don't make costly mistakes.

What types of errors would you make while trading options?

The first error is that you do not schedule your entrances and exits.

Trading options is more complex than trading stocks. When it comes to options trading, there are a lot more things to keep an eye on and be mindful of than when it comes to stock trading. You can't just enter and leave a position in options trading. If you want to benefit while lowering your risks, you'll need to make a lot of changes.

The first error in options trading is to sell without a strategy. What does this mean? You'll start working in the role, and then what? So, what are your plans? Will you let your emotions drive your trading decisions? What happens if the market moves against you? Will you behave as if nothing is happening and shut your eyes like a child until your problems vanish?

Of course, we all know how difficult it is to suppress feelings. However, we also understand that you cannot let your emotions influence your trading decisions. If you do this, your portfolio will blow up and you could lose money.

How do you stop making Mistake?

Simply put, trade more wisely. It's simple to say, but how do you avoid making mistakes in option trading, particularly this one?

Start thinking about how you'll get out. When things aren't going your way, exiting isn't enough just to cut your losses. In any case, you cannot even apply for the job unless you have a strong exit strategy in place. You must prepare ahead of time for your upside and downside exit points. As a result, you're already aware of the price targets. A time frame for each exit is also required, so you must plan ahead.

Keep in mind that options are investments that depreciate over time. The scope of decay increases as the expiration date approaches. Get out of the trade if you're a long call or placed and your goals aren't likely to be met within the planned time frame. Don't waste any time; move on to the next one.

Of course, time will not always betray your trade. Time decay, for example, would benefit you if you sell options without holding them. If time decay erodes the option's price, you'll have a winning trade. For the deal, you'll hold the premium. Yes, whether you sell a call or put the choice for a profit, that's what you'll get. The bad news is that if the deal goes wrong, you might be in for a big loss.

So, it's not a question of what you like or don't like, or what tactic you're using. Each trade must have an exit strategy. Even if you've had a profitable or unsuccessful trade. If your trade is profitable, don't get greedy and keep waiting for more. Profitable exit. If the case is the reverse and the trade is losing, don't wait to leave the losing trade. Waiting for a losing trade to turn around in your favor is too dangerous.

You'll benefit more reliably and will your losses if you have a strategy and know your entry and exit points.

Mistake #1: Relying solely on the long call and long put strategies to make money. When you first start trading options, it's crucial to have a view of what might happen. To put it another way, you'll have to guess, but your calculation must be right. Technical and fundamental analysis, as well as a combination of the two, can be used. You can analyze the volume and price in the charts using technical analysis, and you can also look for support and resistance areas, as well as patterns, to identify buy and sell opportunities. Fundamental analysis can show you a company's financial audits, performance statistics, and current trends, helping you to determine its worth.

You must ensure that the approach you select is structured to take advantage of the outlook you expect when assessing the various options strategies. You must choose which choice is better for your current situation.

Limiting your trades to long call and long put strategies reduces your chances of using more profitable strategies. Furthermore, they are one-of-a-kind, applicable only to options and not to stocks.

How do you stop making mistakes while trading options?

You can exchange an upward or downward move, a move in both directions, or no change while trading options. Furthermore, you can trade an increase in volatility, a decline in volatility, and so on. Is there any reason why you shouldn't incorporate any of these tactics into your trading arsenal?

Of course, not every trader can profit from every option strategy. There are some trading strategies you don't want to use. Perhaps you've had bad luck with them in the past. It is not important to use them, but understanding what they are can be helpful. Simply test the latest technique in a limited sample size. This would not raise the cost per exchange, however, new strategies can be interesting, and you can discover your next favorite strategy as a result.

Mistake #2: You take too long to repurchase a short-term plan.
This technique has the potential to be disastrous. You must be prepared to buy back short strategies as soon as possible. For example, it's easy to love fanfare when a trade is going your way, but the trade might easily go the other way.
We've learned a lot of reasons why traders are taking such a long time to buy back options they've sold. Some people were betting that the deal would expire worthlessly, others didn't want to pay the commission to get out of the positions, and some were just greedy and wanted to make more money from the trade. The list of justifications is lengthy.

How do you make sure you don't make any mistakes while trading options?

If a short option expires and you want to repurchase it, simply do so. Don't be reluctant. There's a rule of thumb to follow. Consider buying it back easily if you can keep 80 percent or more of the initial profit from the sale. A short choice, on the other hand, can come back to bite you if you wait too long to close the place.
Let's put it this way. For example, suppose you sold a short strategy for $2 and now have the opportunity to buy it back for $1 a week before the expiration date. Accept it! It is very unlikely that an extra week of risk is worth it.

Mistake #3: You are purchasing options that are out-of-the-money.
This is a common occurrence among new traders. In the beginning, almost everybody tried it. The explanation is self-evident. Out-of-pocket options are the cheapest, and it seems that starting with them is a good idea. Ok, they're that cheap for a cause, as we discovered later. These options have a very slim chance of being profitable. The majority of the time, they are made useless. Trading these choices is much like playing the lottery, where you have to purchase a lot of tickets in order to find one that pays off and helps you to break even.
When purchasing these options, you must be precise in both timing and direction. And if you keep these options for a longer period of time, moving in the right direction would not benefit you. With expiration approaching, these options have a lower risk of being profitable. It's more likely that they'll stay affordable.

How do you stop making this error?

At the money or in the money, try to get long calls or long puts. Since the options will be more expensive than the out-of-the-money alternative, this will increase their value. As a result, the chances of success will increase, and it will be worth money.

Mistake #4: Doubling up to make up for prior defeats.
There are some unbreakable laws that all traders must follow. If a deal goes against you, they're doing fine. Every trader has gone through something similar. Almost everybody had to deal with a trade that didn't go as planned. The first reaction is to disregard all previously established trading rules and proceed to trade the same choice with which they began.
Have you used the phrase "doubling up to catch up"? However, it is listed as stock trading. For example, if you liked the stock at $50, you'll like it even more at $30 because the lower price would allow you to buy more shares. In the world of options trading, this is irrelevant. It's one of the most common options trading blunders.

Are you making this error?

The doubling up strategy isn't appropriate for options trading. It is not to be used. Option rates do not shift in the same direction as the underlying stock because they are derivatives.
Yeah, this approach will reduce the total cost per deal, but it also raises the risks. So, if a trade goes against you, simply ask yourself, "Is this a trade I want to execute?" So, what are your options in this situation? To avoid losing money, simply close the trade and look for another opportunity. Simply put, it is better to take a loss now rather than wait and suffer larger losses later.
In the world of options trading, anybody can make a mistake. They can be expensive, especially if you are trading low-cost options.

Success Stories to Keep you Inspired

As far as we can tell, options are one of the most flexible instruments in the financial market and seem to be gaining acceptance. When there are more choices available, the success stories are bound to become more frequent. This is not an ordinary rag to riches story, it is amazing. Options trading calls for sound judgment and market savvy but carries considerable risk. as one's character and mentality also have an effect on one's trading performance Here are some inspiring success stories.

Blair Hull recognizes when to take advantage of his good fortune

Addressed by many as one of the New Market Wizards, Blair Hull is best known for his financial strategies as an Options trader that catapulted him to success. Recognized for having executed one of the 40 greatest trades of all times and one of the 25 smartest traders, his net worth is at $400 million as per 2015 data.

He started working at 19 years of age. He started off with a position in a canning factory and later served the US Army as an instructor. Eventually, he went to Las Vegas and worked on the blackjack tables. From there, he made his way to CBOT in Chicago and then created his own trading algorithms that were applied in options space and led to his overall success.

He founded the Hull Trading Company in 1985 and sold it to Goldman Sachs in 1999 valued at $531 million. The firm is known as much for its quantitative new-age trading methodologies as for the reach and the speed. It trades across nine nations and twenty-eight exchanges. But he did not rest with that. Ketchum Trading was his next venture in 1999, and it facilitated trading in futures and options. The Hull Tactical Asset Allocation in 2013 was the latest and enabled algorithmic trading in an advanced manner in the futures.

Hull's Financial Strategies

Hull is best known for his trading coup in 1987. Though he built his electronic trading firm much after this, it is the trade that catapulted him to success. In his own words, Hull likes to think about it as an opportunity where "I was in the right place at the right time" But we do understand that it is his modesty speaking. He came across a panic-stricken trader during the Black Monday in 1987 when the market crashed. That trader offered him 150 futures contracts at an unbelievable price and the rest, as they say, is history.

The twelve indicators are the core backbone of his trading strategy. This strategy is built on the premise that a specific collection of macro-economic indicators and technical pointers can help predict future returns over a medium-term period. These indicators are rather commonplace and easy to follow like the PE ratio, moving averages, inflation readings, and the like. This model operates with two core objectives, better the market indices and cut down the drawdown.

This strategy is back-tested every twenty days to improve its hit ratio. Most of these indicators are predictive to a certain extent and when combined can help you time the market, however improbable that sounds.

Pran Katariya – A Full-time Options Trader

This is another well-known hero of popular options trading success stories who started as a Chemical Engineer and is also a Chartered accountant. His main trading methodology is about creating an income strategy that helps generate a steady inflow of funds for the investor for the maximum possible days. According to him, these income strategies can help one earn close to 2-3% every month, but one should not rubbish it as too small. When you take the per annum picture, these could aggregate to about 42% returns every year and this alone can help double one's money in two years.

He began dabbling in shares early on and started full-time in 2005. But, this was a period where he would trade for 2-3 months, lose more than 30,000, and then recuperate losses by not trading for a period. He realized something was amiss and undertook intensive training in the US.

It was here that he learned options and the common strategies that helped extract maximum gains. It also helped him gain a psychological edge. Once back in India, he realized that the strategies in India had to be adapted to be Indian conditions because of the margin policies. It rendered many of the otherwise successful international strategies useless.

Why he Chose the Weirdor Strategy

He focuses mainly on strategies that ensure steady income every month, and that is why Weirdor or the Jeep strategy is what he uses most commonly. The name is derived from the sharp pay-off graph that looks like a jeep.

Another advantage of the strategy is that the breakeven is wider, and the intra-day market volatility does not affect the trade that much. This is also a cost-effective and simple-to-follow strategy. Depending on whether the market is moving up and down, it is possible to make minor adjustments and come away with a 50-60% profit.

As a rule, he never waits for expiry and exits his positions at least seven days in advance. Most of his trades come with 80% winning assurance and he aims to encourage traders to avoid short-term trade. The objective is either not to lose or lose really small.

Conclusion

When you understand the essential principles, alternatives do not have to be difficult to comprehend. When used correctly, options can provide resources, but when used incorrectly, they can be negative.

This book is jam-packed with knowledge designed to help you properly prepare to trade stocks and, in particular, options using technical analysis. Trading is an operation, and the more prepared you are and the more practice you get, the better you will be at it. Trading is, without a doubt, an undertaking in which you must have confidence. Trust in your ability to complete this task can provide fuel when you need it, visible challenges when you encounter them, and keep you focused on what matters most. Your learning curve would be accelerated if you have confidence. Lack of trust, on the other hand, can be one of the most damaging qualities for a trader's mentality. How would you rebound and refocus if you suffer a setback? What happens if you lose two, three, or four times in a row? Will you have any doubts about your scheme, trading strategy, or skill set?

As all eyes can see, a lack of trust is harmful, while having confidence increases our chances of success. Even if we understand this conceptually or intellectually, our behaviors sometimes tell a different story. So, how do we foster trading confidence? What should we do to instill unwavering confidence in our abilities? Will doing specific things help us build a base that allows us to benefit consistently?

Yeah, you will undoubtedly increase your faith in yourself and your skills.

Will it be sufficient? I'm not sure, but it's a good place to begin.